CREATIVE WAYS WITH MONEY

WHAT YOU CAN DO TO
PROTECT AND ENHANCE YOUR SAVINGS

Jennifer Lancaster

Power of Words

Creative Ways with Money
Copyright © 2020 Jennifer Lancaster

Cover designer: teamjunho
Edited by: Sarah Lancaster

All rights reserved. No part of this book may be reproduced in any form by any electronic or mechanical means including photocopying, recording, or information storage and retrieval without permission in writing from the author.

Creative Ways with Money: 978-0-9945105-4-9 (softback)

Disclaimer: This book is written as an educational guide only and does not constitute financial or legal advice. While every effort has been taken to ensure all material is correct and up-to-date, the author accepts no legal responsibility for errors or omissions. Each individual's situation is different, and all readers should seek professional consultation before embarking on a financial plan. The author accepts no legal responsibility for the performance of any budgeting tools suggested herein. The author does not receive any commissions or benefits from any organisations mentioned.

Publisher: www.powerofwords.com.au/books
Email: jennifer@jenniferlancaster.com.au
Blog: jenniferlancaster.com.au/blog

Published by Power of Words, Clontarf, Queensland, Australia.

Contents

Preface .... *i*

1. What's Wrong with Our Financial System? 1
2. The Fall-out of Sales Influence... 7
   What Can We Learn? 10
3. Mastering Your Negative Emotions When Investing 13
   Going Against the Tide... 14
   What to Look for When Investing 15
   Terrible Experiences to Learn From 20
4. What Has Being Creative got to do with Money?............. 25
   Early Beliefs about Money.. 26
   Using a Creative Mindset for Your Benefit 27
   Find your Life Potential.. 28
   Overcome Limiting Beliefs 29
   Achieving our Highest Goals.. 32
5. Why the Fascination with Crypto-Currency?................... 35
   Another Type of Crypto Exchange 39
   Other Creative Ways to Exchange
     Services and Products.. 40
   Lending to Peers.. 42
6. In Search of Income 45
   Don't Hit the Income Ceiling on Your Way Up................ 48
   You, a Vlogger? Why Not?! 51
   Develop Yourself with Training and Education 53
   Build Your Personal Brand Authority 53
7. Find your Hidden Bank Vault, with Unclaimed Funds.... 55

    What Happens with Unclaimed Bank Accounts?............ 55
    Other Types of Money Claims... 56

8. Fearful Investors 59

9. You: An Empowered Investor 67
    Investing in Company Shares (Stocks).............................. 67
    Exchange Traded Funds (ETFs) and Index Funds........... 68
    Do your Due Diligence... 70

10. Property Investing Outside-the-Box 75
    Property Markets Move in Each Direction 76
    Why Not Negative Cash Flow?.. 77
    Why Not Invest Heavily in Residential Property? 79
    Why Commercial Property? 80

11. Spending Less and Saving $10,000 85
    Spending Tracker Apps... 87
    How Much Should I Save? 88

12. Pick Your Cash-Flow Quadrant 93
    Outside the Quadrant? 95

13. Earning 'Passive Income'/Affiliate Income 99
    Steering Clear of the Gurus 100
    Doing a Simple 'Side Hustle' 101
    Let's Talk More About Business Brand 108
    Long Term Business Thinking... 109
    Niche in your Area of Expertise 109
    How to Build an Audience the Authentic Way.............. 111
    Generating Leads Online 112
    Don't Struggle Alone... 113

14. Design your Life Goals by the Number 115
    Track your Life Goals.. 117

15. Don't Worry, Age is Just a Number 121
    Creating Income from a Farm Property 124

16. Some Easy Ways to Save Money 127
    Turn Around Billing Errors 127
    The Banks' Sob Story 128
    Fight the Fees when Overseas... 129

Conclusion 132

Acknowledgements 134

Endnotes.. 135

Preface

This book is about protecting your money, your capital... before enhancing your savings with investing. Firstly, I want you to become an aware consumer and investor. For that, we have some stories from experts. Expert scammers, that is! While we all can learn something from their tricks, there's a bigger reason for these stories.

It seems to me that the less we know about investing or business, the more we rely on the systems and knowledge of others 'in the trade'. Unfortunately, scammers or spruikers or gurus rely on this ignorance, along with exploiting our human weaknesses.

Protecting ourselves from being ripped off when investing will allow our savings to grow—rather than dwindle. It stands to reason that, knowledge of the common traps of the novice investor or business starter will help keep your growing money pile safe. But it's not that easy. Online scams don't seem like a scam at the outset. And the 'money pits'—institutions where we invest our cash in the hopes that our wealth grows—are even harder to recognise.

Steering clear of 'simple' passive income schemes, we talk about the basics needed to start a side business that becomes a source of fulfilment (and income). Again, it's something to consider from a realistic perspective.

Once you come to realise that all your finances start with you, then your intentions and actions may well change. You can operate your money life less from emotions like fear, greed, and anxiety and more from a planning perspective. After sacrificing a little and putting savings aside, your options open up: you can take the trodden path or invest money in ways that most people don't consider.

To match the promise in the book's title, there are many new tips and tools to help with your money life. I'll be sharing rewarding apps, investing apps, or tips to save money that I found useful. This is so you can see the value of different ideas and perhaps try one or two out.*

Despite there being more financial books from men in powerful positions than women in the Amazon top 20, there are plenty of female authors willing to make you think. For example, Jane Slack-Smith, Nicole Pedersen-McKinnon, Margaret Lomas, and my humble self: many Aussie women have embraced the challenge of boosting financial literacy. And who better to relate to Mums and Dads in middle Australia than women from different walks of life.

As more independent authors get read, we open up the eyes of those who seldom read *The Financial Review*, but who still want to get ahead.

Go your own way!

– Jennifer Lancaster

---

* Don't worry! Each has been investigated and does not have hidden persuasion. However, you should always ensure you're comfortable to give your email address to a company before doing so. You can set up a free GMail account just for doing odd things like this.

1.

What's Wrong with Our Financial System?

Most ordinary Australians (and other world citizens) hope that the banking and financial services industry is in place to help us make the most of our money while making a fair profit, but not at our expense. Sadly, no. Later, we'll reveal how we can win the battle and cut our banking fees.

One of the main findings of the Royal Commission into Misconduct in the Banking, Financial Services & Superannuation Industry (February 2019) was that the big four banks' staff performance was measured and rewarded based on profits and by pushing sales. This resulted in customers being openly misled. It also found conflicts of interest in the delivery of financial advice; confusion about the roles and responsibilities of mortgage brokers; and issues with the way banks deal with Indigenous communities.[1]

This comes on top of initial allegations that certain banks received fees from deceased customers, charged fees for financial advice that customers never received, and then hid all this from the regulators.

You could say a lot of us were outraged at these findings. I certainly was. In this environment, it seems there are better ways for consumers to save, lend, and grow their wealth than relying on the financial services industry.

Due to the Royal Commission and to protect the interests of the people, our parliament had to act. Federal Treasurer, Josh Frydenberg, declared in February 2019 that the Australian government would take action on all 76 recommendations of the Banking Royal Commission—with a focus on restoring lost trust in the financial system, while maintaining credit flow.[2]

The Commission's recommendations seek to change dodgy tactics, like selling funeral insurance to the vulnerable. It will also put the onus on banks to help those in remote areas to access suitable banking services. Mortgage Brokers were also put under the microscope. Trailing commission and volume bonuses were set to be cut, but this particular recommendation was instantly met with push-back from independent brokers, with one petition registering 78,000 votes in a month. This cut has now been moderated so that brokers can continue as an essential part of our lending system.

There has been a long banking industry history of unfair conduct when dealing with overdrafts to Australian farmers. Now, along with helping farmers by providing a national scheme for farm debt mediation, banks will be restricted from charging default interest on loans when farmland is affected by natural disaster—like drought. In the 1990s and 2000s, the big banks foreclosed on many farms far too soon.

A little over a decade ago, the credit expansion left Mum and Dad and retiree investors open to exploitation. It was quite common then to invest in shares or funds using the equity in your own property. Storm Financial, a financial planning company that allowed people on low incomes to double gear (margin loan and home loan), raking in 7 percent in fees while doing so, went into liquidation in 2009.

Storm clients lost $800 million collectively from both poor advice and margin lending calls brought about by the falling sharemarket. Commonwealth Bank, a major supplier of these home equity loans, did not stop people nearing the end of their working lives from getting into unrepayable debts. But once outed, the Commonwealth did allow loan forgiveness on some of those huge losses, of $136 million and $132 million.[3]

Why?

Why is it that if the law is not clearly made for the consumer, and regulators like ASIC (Australian Securities and Investments Commission) and APRA (Australian Prudential Regulation Authority) are too lenient, the people behind greedy institutions will get away with taking millions of dollars before they are found out?

In Australia, some financial telemarketing companies were selling insurance policies to the mentally disabled or those in remote communities. These were people who did not understand why they were buying insurance or that they would be liable for ongoing deductions from a pension. These unethical practices are not something you would expect from corporations that have had decades of billion-dollar profits (and reputation building).

Think about your own bank statements: overdue fees, over-limit fees, overdrawn fees, dishonours, high levels of credit card interest… is it in your favour, or the bank's? Most likely, the banks. Millions of dollars in trailing fees were going to the benefit of those in the financial services industry... all while some personal superannuation funds or retirement pensions went backwards from administrative fees and insurance.

So, it's certainly time to make our own rules to protect our savings and get ahead.

Second in the world for personal debt levels, Australia's Household Debt is 120 percent of Gross Domestic Product. Individually, 37 percent of us are struggling to pay off our debts. With triple the debt burden of 28 years ago and more of our income going to paying debt, it's no surprise that interest rate cuts are not having a positive effect on consumer spending.[4]

Getting off the debt treadmill is one of the main things to work on in our personal finances.

Are you also trying to build up your retirement savings? It hasn't been easy with those unwanted life insurance premiums or 'performance' fees on superannuation funds that don't ever perform above average. That's why we must look at industry funds, benchmarks, and the performance of our own fund against the benchmark.

The Productivity Commission's landmark review of Superannuation found a significant number of underperforming funds in the market. Being in one of these dogs could cost a member an average of $188,000 after a full working life. Retail funds were found to be the worst for the impact of fees. The commission forced all APRA-regulated funds to carry out an annual outcome test across their portfolios. (APRA is the regulator for the retail fund industry).

If investment options fall short of their stated benchmark by more than half a percentage point a year over a rolling eight-year period, then the fund would have 12 months to sharply lift performance before it faced closure.[5]

Why wait for that, though? Your Super fund is yours to nurture, and you should. We'll discuss this later, in the chapter: *Age is just a number*.

Before we move on, let's take a short lesson from history. It's always amazing to me what crazy things happen inside corporations that then affect the lives of ordinary people.

What's Wrong with our Financial System?

2.

The Fall-out of Sales Influence

It was 2006 and Brad Cooper had just been jailed for five years on 13 counts of bribery and corruption. Bankrupt and overweight, gone were the heady days of well-paid speaking gigs at motivational seminars, admiring the view from his chosen waterfront property (he had two), nightclubbing, or riding around in his Ferrari.[6]

It seems that Mr Bradley Cooper had bribed HIH executive Bill Howard to show favour to Mr Cooper's company, Home Security International. HIH was then a giant in the insurance industry. The bribe allowed Brad to squeeze out another $11 million from HIH, shortly before its $5.3 billion collapse in 2001—the largest ever collapse in Australia's corporate history.

This was just the tip of an influence iceberg that started with Cooper's determination to have the help of Rodney Adler at FAI. He wanted him to be venture capitalist for his company. Just as he schmoozed Rodney, he allied himself later with CEO Ray Williams (because they both came from poor upbringings and 'hustled' their way up). Cooper mesmerised and influenced others, according to Andrew Main, through his ability to "establish facts by a mixture of talking, confusing people's recollections, extracting promises and drafting letters".[7]

Cooper's ability to calmly handle huge risk was in conflict with the insurance game, which for good reason is about sensible re-insurancing and keeping risks low. Despite his salesman and speaker background, he wheedled his way into the huge corporate player, HIH, extracting money to aid the cash flow of his own much smaller company.

HIH's long-running CEO, Ray Williams; Cooper's friend and FAI executive, Rodney Adler, and Brad Cooper were found to be equal parties in major corporate crime. They were all convicted on corporate criminal charges. After serving two and a half years, Adler walked free on 13 October 2007, ready to face NSW civil charges over recommending big bonuses to executives before OneTel failed.[7]

You can read the whole sordid story in the book, *Other People's Money*, by Andrew Main.

Magic Sales Tactics

It was 1998 or so when I witnessed a much younger, trimmer, and more energetic Bradley Cooper in action at a marketing seminar. The well-paid talk centred around creating 'magic moments' for customers, and it obviously worked. FAI Home Security grew incredibly fast to become a top seller of home security alarm systems.

Brad started out when he was 18 years old, in Perth, selling clothes. He bought a men's jeans store with a loan from a wealthy bookmaker. He bought another two stores, before selling them to a retailer for $200,000. "He repaid the bookmaker, and there was no turning back".[6]

The sales tactics mentioned by Cooper in his marketing speech included a comparison technique psychologists call 'price anchoring': meaning the tendency to rely on the first piece of information offered when making buying decisions.

In his story, a customer in a men's clothing store is shown a high-priced suit (e.g. $1,000) and then a more affordable, lower-priced suit. That way, the lower-priced suit seems a bargain, especially if the salesperson points out that certain features remain. Cooper was enamoured with this approach.

Without stating it, he mentioned the 'foot-in-the-door' approach too, where a salesperson asks for a little favour and this compliance helps to get a yes to the bigger ask later on.

To help with word of mouth, Cooper created 'magic moments' in his home security selling process. A magic moment example was, if I remember correctly, after installing the security system, the installer helped out by changing a light bulb or something else they weren't required to do. Cooper was up with all the tricks of a 'sales pro'.

Cooper's baby, Home Security International (HSI), sold over-priced burger alarms and fire protection kits for $2,200 that were made by others. The alarms were worth maybe $500 wholesale price, but of course salespeople must be paid. The sales agents offered low-earning people in Sydney's west a 'hire purchase' plan for the systems, with interest rates of around 20 percent. Newly-created FAI Finance provided (and profited handsomely from) the offered finance.

Helping the coffers at FAI, in 1997 the security company floated on the American stock exchange and as a major shareholder, FAI made US$23.5 million. FAI's stake in the 'liquid assets' of Home Security kept them propped up financially for several years. In 1998, HIH took over from FAI in paying the bills for Home Security International, eventually snowballing the amount spent on the unrelated company to $80 million.[7]

What Happened After the Sentences?

In October 2010, Brad Cooper walked free from Kirkconnell Prison (NSW), lighter in both debt and body weight. Just nine years after embezzling millions, he was free to start again. He currently proffers his services as a consultant.

FAI boss Rodney Adler went from 2.5 years in prison to being a well-paid consultant and, oddly, lecturing on corporate governance and ethics. He's still a venture capitalist.[8] But hey, it's all fair play, right?

What Can We Learn?

I tell you this old story because it reminds us that big business doesn't always mean ethical or durable business. Sometimes those who exert their personal influence over others wheedle their way into corporations. Fudged or false financial figures are sometimes displayed to the public, all while the company is on a debt-laden rocky ship.

Why do some think it's okay to use their influence to fund their greed? We'll never know, but not everyone in business who becomes insolvent is unethical, by any stretch. Compare what happens in large corporate insolvencies (from unethical conduct) to the average small business owner whose company goes insolvent from poor management. If the small business owner has no assets to pay an insolvency practitioner, they often become personally liable for debts, particularly guaranteed loans. Many suffer terrible anxiety and humiliation along with this bankruptcy. Without lending and assets, few return to a place where they can operate a cash-flow-happy business.

If, like me, you believe in the best in people, you've probably been a scam victim. Two decades ago, I was victim to that old 'social proof' investing con: 'your friend is investing in this, so why don't you get in…? You can't lose'. The swindle involved buying a speculative biotech company in North America (not one on the NASDAQ, but a much smaller market), and basically, not letting you sell it. The fake stockbrokers were persistent and thankfully, I did not say yes to a second and a third conning attempt (by a different company) ten years later.

It's through this and other painful experiences that I learned how to master my emotions when investing or when learning from gurus. Perhaps it's time for you to also master your emotions for when you might meet with 'opportunity' from others?

The Fall-out of Sales Influence

3.
Mastering Your Negative Emotions When Investing

Those who are swept along by the tide of enthusiasm for a new technology that's going to be huge, a launching IPO, or a salesperson's wondrous spiel, fail to consider that their initial emotions (and hope for the magic answer) cannot be trusted. You may think, "no way, I'm no sucker", but one of those evil twins (fear or greed) will surely come out whenever your mind is tricked into thinking that 'this new opportunity is a sure thing'.

Greed gets its hooks into us through the euphoria and hope incited by the seminar spruiker's spiel, but fear is lurking there too.

Why would you jump into the latest initial coin offering (ICO) or initial public offer (IPO)? Fear of missing out.

Why would you hold onto that stock that has only ever sunk since you bought it? Fear of making the loss real.

Why would you do a property investing course but not apply for a property within the framework and budget? Analysis paralysis—or fear of making a mistake.

Why would you stay in a home loan with a lousy interest rate at a big bank? Perhaps fear of change or worry over your credit record.

On that last point, my family dallied in the changing of home loans, paying 1.25% p.a. more than most others. Considering that the mortgage style (offset) had helped us in bad times, and that it's a little trickier to qualify when having your own business, there was a mental wall to climb. Climbing that wall meant finding another reason to change the mortgage… and the reason was that it benefited my husband's business. Changing loans meant we got an emergency funds back-up for the business and a better interest rate.

It was a good decision, because even with a fixed interest rate and yearly fee, it turned out to be a win that is now saving us $2,000 a year in bank interest. Key to changing our loan was researching the interest rates available and seeing what features those lower-rate loans have.

Take a look at the interest rates you are being charged on your mortgage account and any store or credit card. Does it meet the market today?

Going Against the Tide

While going against the tide of opinion is a fine idea to make more wealth in a downturn, there is a reason that most of us can't easily practise contrarian investing. Contrarians invest when others are running scared and hold back when a market is bubbling with hot activity. The reason that it's hard to do this is because we learn about the world from others and generally accept what others are doing or saying as correct… and because we want to be accepted and liked ourselves, called normative social influence.

The psychological aspects of informational and normative

social influence means that we find it hard to go against the majority when investing.

Using the critical analysis tips in this book means you will be on the lookout and try to break the spell of social influence. You'll invest only when and where you believe it's right for you. This 'breaking the spell' also applies to network marketing opportunities.

Many people call this ability to intuit the truth and take stock emotional intelligence. Emotional intelligence, or EQ, has nothing to do with finite intelligence; it is more the ability to perceive a person's true mood, motivations and desires. In our case, it is taking a breath and doing some research before jumping in. It is being strategic with decisions. Honing this set of skills will help you become a better investor and a better business manager.

You can pair this intuition and questioning assumptions with creative thinking, such as I'll show you in the 'property investing outside-the-box' chapter.

Creative with Money rule #1: Don't believe the voice of greed, don't follow others; invest to your own clear aims.

What to Look for When Investing

Those who have conquered the twin evils of greed and fear—and also mastered the art of ignoring the majority—seem to do very well in stockmarket investing. George Soros, Warren Buffett and Charlie Munger are three such people. Warren Buffett and his partner Charlie Munger have high EQ when it comes to decisions, and you can pick up their best-selling books to garner more on their insights at any bookstore (if you can manage the weight!)

Many would-be investors start their journey off by desiring a nice, solid capital gain. They forget all about regular income and longevity. Most only see the surface. For example, many US investors thought Uber Tech would be a great buy, based on future technology plans and news hype. This is like thinking the tip of the iceberg is the part the captain needs to watch out for!

In 2019, Uber Technologies Inc's initial public offering (IPO) launched at US$45, but ended the day down, at US$41.57.[9] It is now $30.17 and has zero dividend yield. Time will tell whether Uber Tech can find a profitable division to outweigh other large, loss-making ones. It seems the traders did not believe it is a fantastic bet after all.

Uber Technologies is losing $1 billion each year as it jumps from one industry to the next. This loss happened despite its 2013 to 2017 operating practices of pillaging contractors from competitors and ignoring local laws.

Though currently making this yearly loss, in one documentary a financial expert said that Uber (to survive) needs to be valued at $90 Billion.[10] Certainly, no company can last for long making a continual loss.

Remember the concept of normative influence? Because some of us believe other investors have the answer, we buy into widespread hype. Not so my high-school-aged daughter: straight away she understood that Uber are putting out fancy videos on new technologies (flying cars) to build the hype, not because it will prove a winning play. When someone is guided by logic and foresight rather than emotion, it takes little time to discern the 'real story' behind the news.

You can bring this real-world view to any investment offering, particularly that of cybercurrencies and new technologies. Initial Coin Offerings (ICOs), for instance, do not let you have an ownership or shareholder status, so in effect you do not have any claim to future profits. ICOs have been used to raise hundreds of millions of dollars for blockchain-related projects, often with limited information about their goals. Further, when buying a crypto coin or token, you are not buying an income stream, to state the obvious.

Watch the Madness of Crowds

Bitcoin-style launches sometimes mimic the Tulip bulb mania in the 1630s. You see, it's not about a technology advance at all; booms are based on the 'madness of crowds'. As the crowd gets whiff of a good profit from early investors, they clamour to get on board (never mind the risks). This buying madness continues until some sensible people report that it's all based on lies, hype, or fantasy.

You can see how Dutch Tulip bulb mania of the 1630s took the price sky high in the chart below… in a similar way to how new tech or cryptocurrencies do today.

On Google, you can look up the Bitcoin to Australian dollar trading price. Notice how it moved from $12,766 to $10,766 in just one month, November to December 2019. We can only speculate where it will go next.

Mastering Your Negative Emotions When Investing

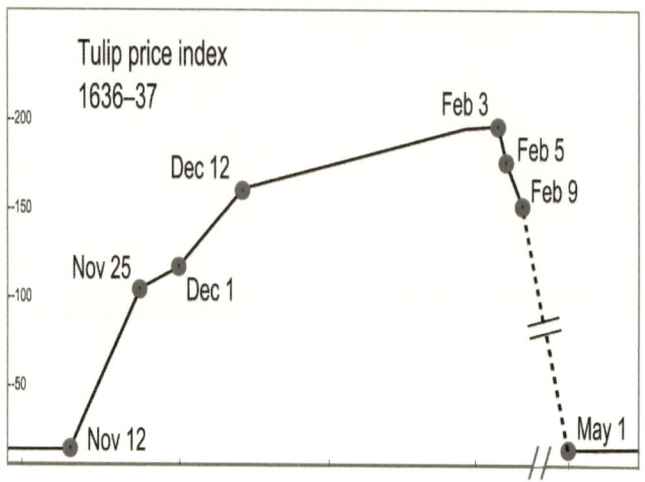

Figure 1 A standardized price index for tulip bulb contracts, created by Earl Thompson.
Chart by By JayHenry - Own work from data of Thompson, CC BY-SA 3.0

A Gouda Tulip bulb (as a futures contract) ascended to about 2,000 Guilders and sold for 1/10th of a Guilder a century later

Dutch Tulip bulb markets, Bitcoin or its clones, or the latest space-age company all seem to suffer the same trajectory: hype, boom, then crash. Perhaps that's because their worth is not based on intrinsic value.

A tulip bulb has an intrinsic value of a few dollars. Houses also have intrinsic value (perhaps the replaceable value). However, people can't do much with cryptocurrency unless others agree it is worth something.

These examples seem the very opposite of 'value investing', which is investing in companies that have a growing value, solid profits and good management. In hindsight, the Bitcoin clones go against the economic measure of value as: 'scarcity and utility'.

An original Bitcoin perhaps has scarcity value because there is a limited number available, but not much utility. When was the last time you were asked for Bitcoin in a coffee shop?

One journalist pointed out that the value of the people network of Bitcoin has value. The theory is, the more people using the currency, even for coin trades, the more value the network holds. Others think these currencies might replace a small portion of the stored gold, which is also favoured by big investors.[11]

You can't see quite see the end of Bitcoin yet, but the full cycle can take some time. The tipping point in a boom-bust cycle usually comes when the majority of people realise that what was believed is not going to come to pass.

The bumps and pits of Bitcoin's rivals—Ethereum, Ripple's XRP, Litecoin and Bitcoin Cash—also affect the price of Bitcoin. Trading coins on a futures market seems to add even more risk to the risk equation. (Futures trading is akin to betting on the future price of a commodity, or in this case, a coin).

The hype and promises involved in new technology or new networks is never sustainable; only awesome products and valuable services that benefit all are. What comes to mind is Amazon, the company. Not many authors mind if Amazon takes a cut, because they are allowing us to earn money from our ideas by providing the world's largest marketplace to sell it on. Plus, there are still other options available.

In contrast, restaurants and cafes are feeling the pinch of platforms like Uber Eats and MenuLog taking around a 30 percent cut. This is because the owners have to pay a lot of costs already and meal prices must remain the same. Restaurant & Catering

Industry Association figures estimate that average profit margins at Australian restaurants have sunk from about 10%, before meal delivery companies arrived in Australia, to between 2-4% in 2019.[12]

The best way to support restaurants is by directly going there to eat.

Unfortunately, the crypto-currency market has been built on a new kind of hype. Crypto-currency writers encourage people that these digital coins will avoid bank greed and help them trade continually upwards. Like many types of investment trade, from future silver prices to Contracts for Difference, the risks of trading in any type of crypto for its own sake... is high.

While some traders got into Bitcoin early and made a tidy profit, this doesn't lower the risk of trading in these currencies. Timing is always a safety hazard when trading and speculating.

Terrible Experiences to Learn From

Over the years, I have felt the pull of FOMO (Fear of Missing Out) or FFI (Fear of Failing in Investment). Once, I mistimed the economic cycle because I so wanted it to be true that the commodities boom was not fizzling. And this was after I put a picture of the economic clock (and its ever-changing cycle) in my earlier book!

Looking at the stellar growth of the recent past and thinking it would last tripped me up there. But the economic cycle keeps on ticking round, despite my poor lack of timing.

Another time, I bought $1,000 of Retail Food Group (RFG) shares at $2.49. It seems I caught 'a falling knife', or bought because it was cheaper than previous times. The management claimed that they were still strong. Then all the bad news came piling out about disgruntled Dunkin Donuts and Gloria Jeans franchisees and poor sales. The franchises were failing. My shares dropped all the way down to 50 cents, where I stopped checking it (having not set a 'stop loss' price: another mistake). An email came from RFG to offer me a new share issue at 10 cents each, effectively diluting my holding. Ouch!

You see, there is often a very good reason for a company's shares to dip, whether it's insiders talking about company problems or waves in the external market to the company. So do your research.

A stop loss is a set price (set when buying), which can limit the loss to 10-20 percent. When the share price is hit, the automated order sells your share. The technical part comes in choosing a percentage that will not trigger the loss on weekly ups-and-downs, as that may mean you have to pay two brokerage fees and buy it again as quickly as possible.

It's hard, but we learn by making mistakes. During my research over the years, I noticed that finance companies launching dud products often invest in glossy brochures or videos with celebrity endorsements and other forms of social proof selling—all while failing to provide any actual foundation of value.

Returns in the form of gain and income is how we measure value. One scam cryptocurrency-trading scheme claimed up to 1% daily (365% yearly) returns. Naturally, this is ludicrous, and it turned out to be a Ponzi scheme.

If you're clever with your retirement account allocation, your fund might gain 20 percent over a very good year (less fees) but that's about the best scenario.

There are plenty of other scams around to rob you. One crazy scam I read about was involved with getting your nest egg early. Scamwatch.gov.au says, "Superannuation scams offer to give you early access to your super fund, often through a self-managed super fund or for a fee." Agreeing on a hardship story, as your 'financial advisor', they contact your super fund and get them to release your superannuation (to them). Once released, the scammer takes a large chunk out of that amount, perhaps leaving you with nothing at all.

On compassionate grounds, yes, you can access your personal superannuation funds before 60 years of age, but those who offer you early access are doing so illegally.

Remember, it is saved for retirement for a reason… because the Aged Pension is fairly low. And if you do happen to die before this maturation date, then your next of kin is usually set to receive your superannuation anyway.

Greed is summed up by the attitude many novice investors take during a general market boom. They are cocksure and proud of their gains. Some go 'all in' and leverage to the hilt. When booms happen, rather than congratulate yourself on a sterling investment choice, you can say to yourself:

> 'A rising tide lifts all boats.'

This means that when the sharemarket (or gold market or property market) is rising in a bullish way, it's pretty easy to latch onto a boat and make nice profits. But look out for when the tide turns… and it always does.

Don't let fear be your enemy; let it be the signal you sense from your watch-tower of the super ego. *Ah, I recognise that fear of making a mistake with my carefully analysed path: I'm not going to let that overcome me!*

Mastering Your Negative Emotions When Investing

4.
What Has Being Creative got to do with Money?

Using creative ways with money is not necessarily investing in new currencies or tech plays. It's certainly not creating passive income from ripping people off by selling them over-priced houses, schemes, or high-level investing memberships. Being creative with money is not being a clever salesperson who offers poor value to the customer.

Although we're revealing sad setback stories to learn particular lessons, there is an upside. Money seems to flow more to those with a huge value to give, generosity, and a win-win mindset. The scam artists and slick types might rake in a few million, but without a good moral code, that wealth does not stick around. Witness the likes of Nathan Tinkler, once a mining magnate, or our old friend, Bradley Cooper.

We all have emotions around money—it is not simply a means of exchange. Take away our ability to earn and we don't just think about the loss of work; our prime concern is how to pay for things we need, and then, how to otherwise exchange our time for money. By only having the negative emotions of fear, greed, or anxiety about investing or earning, this leads us into all kinds of problems.

The more we worry about lack of money, the less creative we are in this area. It's not about simple numbers either; will extra money help you buy things you cherish, or enjoy doing? Or will it just lead to more spending to keep up with appearances?

I want you to prepare yourself for a better future with the use of your creative imagination and further research. On the right side of the brain, creative brainstorming will fuel your imagination, that powerhouse Einstein alluded to. Tangible payoffs of this may include: better ideas to use at work; more innovation in the start-up or growth stage of business; ideas to further your own personal brand and influence; and of course, more money in the bank.

Using the left side of the brain, more awareness of your own triggers and emotions around money concepts may help you become more logical in financial decisions. The left side helps you to analyse every new idea or opportunity through a cost-and-risk versus likely-reward lens.

It's my belief that we need both sides of our brain working on our professional development and our finances, and not lean too heavily on one side or the other.

Early Beliefs about Money

The way we grew up to think about money, saving and investing is interesting. Think about the phrases 'the filthy rich'; 'Scrooge', and from the Bible, 'the love of money is the root of all evil'. But what if I said money can help people's lives? It can help you and your family's life.

A fluid income can also help others, like students, poor

children, the sick, and others who have had it tough.

Which of those two viewpoints do you really agree with? It might be time to upgrade your operating system around money.

Here's another concept: creating money comes from your time, energies and imagination. This means that you don't have to have large amounts of capital right now... but you do need an open and creative mindset.

Using a Creative Mindset for Your Benefit

Some people, as they age, get quite narrow in mindset, with limited ability to step outside of what's considered 'normal work' or 'usual investment'. Others find a way to keep open to new ideas and solutions to their problems. A creative mindset is one where you are open to the opportunities and possibilities in your life.

Practising daily, you'll start to relish the creative process and innovative thinking.

Everyone can access creative thinking: no matter how old or how young. Our Australian Education department is even teaching year 10 students to think critically and creatively.

> *"Creative thinking involves students learning to generate and apply new ideas in specific contexts, seeing existing situations in a new way, identifying alternative explanations, and seeing or making new links that generate a positive outcome.*
>
> *This includes combining parts to form something original, sifting and refining ideas to discover possibilities, constructing theories and objects, and acting on intuition." (Australian-curriculum.edu.au)*[13]

One way to bypass your critical analyst is to speed brainstorm on an issue, coming up with as many answers as possible. Pick any topic that may help you to create new business or new income streams. Rely on your first thoughts to come up with as many answers as possible within five minutes. Then call up your critical analyst to choose the best two. Look more into these and connect to whichever also resonates with your own passions.

Find your Life Potential

Some people spend 50 hours a week doing a job (or getting to that job) that they now don't like. Life is finite. If that 50 hours is making you miserable, overweight, stressed, and time poor, then you might find this next exercise very valuable.

To find quality ideas for your next career move—in alignment with what you really want—take some time to draw an Ikigai diagram. It is also useful for new freelancers and business owners.

A Japanese concept, your 'Ikigai' lies at the centre of the interconnecting circles. This could also be called your 'life potential'. If you are currently drifting without a mission, the finding of this can feel like you found a missing key.

Knowing what you want and what your strengths are forms the basis of your self-worth and the secret to creating extremely good value for others.

Once you truly value your own creative thoughts and actions, you open yourself to new possibilities from a positive framework. The possibilities are all around you, all the time.

CREATIVE WAYS WITH MONEY

Possibilities do not just come in the form of new technologies, like Instagram, but also new concepts. The concept is the more important thing.

Overcome Limiting Beliefs

Writing a book is a personal achievement. Not quite as hard as building a business—but it has its challenges. Many of the new authors I work with are worried over many things and sometimes my job is to help push them over these mental hurdles. Inner talk or worries, such as:

What I'm writing about may garner enemies in certain sectors

What Has Being Creative got to do with Money?

I doubt that anyone will want to read it!
I've no idea how to market the book, so it will probably flop.

These incorrect assumptions can keep people from expressing their truth and pushing forward with their (often educated) perspective. If you fear the finish line, it's hard to even get off the blocks. It's the same with any individual pursuit.

It's likely that none of the bad things you imagine will eventuate... and you can always learn more about marketing and personal brand.

These fears also crop up when pushing outside of our 'normal' to invest and create wealth. Fears pile down on us every time we go to expand: negative self-talk is stopping us going forward. As Dean Graziozi says in *Millionaire Success Habits*, stop listening to the negative news and the fears of your 'inner villain'.

I listened to that villain for about ten years. I let myself off the hook with thoughts like: 'everyone says business is hard', 'the local economy is down', and my unique, self-made doubts. But last year, I decided take my freelance service and add client education to make it a better business. I began to think: what would my authors want? And what do service business owners want?

There were practical hurdles of course. Funding: nothing but what I made. Memory: like a twig. Distractions: plenty. But there are some really good things, like client feedback, creative channels, and a supportive business network, so I decided to focus on those.

Create a New Story

Definitely, some of us have blocks to success that we must just put up with or mitigate; for example, poor eyesight or attention deficit disorder. But the biggest hurdle is always the mental one. So I started to re-write my mental story: the one that says I'm too old, not talented enough, too shy, and not especially intelligent. Isn't it true that we are a harsh critic of ourselves but we don't think of our friends that way?

I think my friend is intelligent, gifted, confident, and often wise. Turning that around, I see our similarities and think: well, why can't that apply to me?

Starting with your own struggle story will help you see the BS that your negative talk is coming up with:

> I am too old… I don't have friends in business… I have no real capital to start… I'm more analytical than creative… I'm not good with finance calculations… I can't organise a thing! Planning is just not me… I have no real point of difference… I don't learn well.

Some of these are labels or assumptions; they're not real. Others are areas which you could learn some of and delegate the rest. What's the price if you don't? Stagnation at best.

A new story will help you be courageous and reach beyond your income comfort zone.

Starting to create a new story about yourself can help form an identity that is more in alignment with where you want to go. That's why, when I give a talk, I try to help change the way the audience looks at marketing: more as a skill and language to be learned than something to be feared.

> *"Marketing is nothing more than clearly and effectively communicating your true value of what you have to the world."*
> *– Jeff Walker, Product Launch Formula.*

Rather than considering yourself as being 'good' or 'bad' at marketing, it's best to think of it as a growth chart:

Achieving our Highest Goals

So, even though we may write down our goals, which is good, the reason we might not achieve our Big Hairy Audacious Goals (BHAG) is because our inner picture of ourselves doesn't align with the kind of person that can hit those goals.

Plus, the things we say don't always align with our goals. (Stop saying you 'can't afford it'). The things we think, you guessed it, many times don't align with our goal. Conversely, aligning everything we do, say, and think is imperative in truly believing in ourselves and achieving our highest goals.

Imposter syndrome is the name given to the feeling of being a fraud, when really, you're doing quite well. Mohammed Ali said, "I am the greatest" many times, so how could his mind believe anything but that thing, when he said it so often. Perhaps you could try it!

At the other end of the spectrum are those who think they are above-average at something… but are not (they don't know what they don't know). This tendency to underestimate or overestimate our abilities is called the *Dunning-Kruger effect*. However, I believe more of us trying to expand our boundaries are at the "low confidence/low knowledge" end of the see-saw than at the other end.

That's self-belief and confidence covered, but what about profits?

Put Your Focus on the Right Things

Getting a good return on time and money invested is important in all pursuits, and this only happens when we focus well. If in business, it's your responsibility to know Profit and Loss at-a-glance and how things could change if you get five more prospects. If involved in property renovations, it's in your interests to know how much the renovation may cost, understand the value of surrounding houses renovated to that level, and input all the other hidden costs, to get a good idea of profit.

So, a Profit and Loss report is surprisingly relevant in many aspects of our lives. What I'm saying here is profits are more likely to be made when we focus on them.

But we often get caught up in learning all the little things and forget the strategy, for instance, learning a new software or learning how to be an influencer. Sometimes these things are foundational for your personal brand, if that's your plan, but more often they're just a small ladder rung, when you could be taking a bigger ladder rung. It's best to think first: what will my new personal brand need? Or, what will my new investor side need most?

After you create your big picture plan, then you can drill down to the smaller steps needed… without getting lost in the schemes and plans of others. Drawing a mind map™ is ideal for this. Google 'Tony Buzan Mind Map' and you'll soon have a plethora of how-to material on their creation.

Then, who can you get to help with some of the smaller steps that aren't your fortè? An intern, a virtual assistant, or even a daughter or son?

You can learn more about just about anything, and it's generally worthwhile if that area is going to make a big impact on your life. Learnings that should make a big impact are:

- Investing strategies and principles, like compound interest, yield, return on cash invested (Internal Rate of Return), effects of the economic cycle
- Business strategy, innovation, and creating digital assets
- Marketing principles, market research, and strategic marketing

Creative with Money rule #2: *Focus on your big picture plan and learn the more crucial strategies before moving onto the small steps.*

5.

Why the Fascination with Crypto-Currency?

The Bitcoin story has not ended. Only new crypto technology successes will write what happens to its value… because what worth does any coin have that cannot be easily and cheaply exchanged for tangible goods?

I'll answer that for you: only a speculative agreement based on what it's worth in the minds of traders. This type of trading is not investing; it is speculating. And when you speculate on things you don't understand the mechanics behind, nor the risk, you can get burned.

Remember, every time a crypto coin traded, you pay a fee to the broker or platform, e.g. at Coinspot this can be 0.1% if putting in a trade order or 1% if an instant order. Deposits also cost, unless using POLI method. The risk doesn't end there. There is also the difference between the price you buy at and the price you sell at.

Many wish they had bought some Bitcoin in year one, but only because its increasing value is built on the hype surrounding cryptocurrency. Because the number of Bitcoin issued is capped at 21 million coins, many people think this means it will trade high forever. But I believe that more practical features must be

Why the Fascination with Crypto-Currency?

created for any particular crypto-currency to be long-lived.

Greed and naivety played a big part in the 2018 collapse of BitConnect, an Indian-founded international cryptocurrency lending investment scheme. At one point it was valued at a cap of U$2.6 billion, bolstered by the huge growth in Bitcoin and its own marketing.

This Bitcoin trading platform collapse is one of many similar schemes/scams. This one used event marketing, digital marketing and MLM (multi-level marketing) affiliates; even using Google-friendly news articles to cover up the problems in Britain and the cease and desist in Texas Securities.[14]

Promoter John Bigatton ran the BitConnect (Australia) sales machine from the Gold Coast. A Channel 7 Sunday Night report on his ex-clients revealed that the salesman used a spreadsheet to 'show' gullible investors that their investment would grow by 1% each day... meaning a $140,000 sum could reach $8 million in a year.[15]

ASIC's Scamwatch states that this kind of return is preposterous, and to promise such a return normally means a scam.

Unphased by his losses, one male victim said that he was still investing some cash into Bitcoin, in an illogical effort to make a bad investment turn good. His female partner gave him dagger eyes as she said she knew nothing of this. Two unfortunate couples shown on the program lost all their life savings to the scam, money which was swallowed up when BitConnect was found to be a 'Ponzi' scheme and collapsed.[15]

A Ponzi scheme is one where ever more money is flowing into the scheme from innocent newbies, going straight to those already invested (as 'returns'), until such time that someone catches on and the whole thing collapses.

In March 2019, OneCoin was found to be a pyramid scheme with no value. It was really a multilevel marketing network where members received commission for recruiting others to buy educational materials (attached to sums of OneCoin). Legitimate cryptocurrency is exchanged with the blockchain: a secure linkage of packets of data. But according to Cryptoslate news, OneCoin cryptocurrency 'did not use a blockchain at all while it scammed investors out of billions'. It could not be used to purchase anything and there was no way to trace any transactions.[16]

OneCoin Ltd claimed to have 3 million members—or victims—worldwide. The multilevel scheme generated over €3.3 billion in fraudulent sales. OneCoin's founder, Konstantin Ignatov, was arrested on March 6, 2019 on wire fraud conspiracy by the United States IRS-Criminal Investigation and the FBI.[17]

This is the problem with investing using real (fiat) dollars in something which cannot be verified to exist, rather than simply trading X this for X that with someone you know. MLM schemes often have recruitment and chasing wealth as the drivers, rather than the exchange of tangible products for money.

With crypto, there is no 'central' point or regulator and the transactions are untraceable through many layers of digital exchange on the blockchain. This is why those scammers who try to blackmail someone with the site logins or passwords they pilfered, often ask for their ransom in Bitcoin.

An anonymous fellow showed us all just how easy it is to fool people online to invest in a worthless token. Calling it Useless Ethereum Token (UET), this person launched a website in mid-

Why the Fascination with Crypto-Currency?

Think Differently - Alan Rowe

"As money is just another form of collaboration and is a means of exchange, it doesn't become valuable until someone has bought it and put a value on it. Encrypted currencies are part of our future, but fiat currency will always be there too.

In a distributed world, closed systems have their limitations. Governments don't want to lose their control over an international currency, but that won't stop any cross-border currency going ahead.

The idea of distributed collaboration is that nobody owns the system or the code. We're moving to a world of crossing borders, as seen in individualised power generation, intellectual property, and open-source code. The nature of this decentralisation allows us to communicate and exchange with anyone, anywhere. So, governments can only regulate the crypto-currencies, not control them.

Don't let your current beliefs, paradigm, and education taint a new way of doing business. Our human problem is that we try to solve our problems mentally—without any information. Think of the words 'blockchain', 'open source', or 'decentralisation'; find out what these are all about rather than guessing. Then you will be able to change the way you act in the world.

I succeed and so do you, and the person next to you.

Competition does not exist in a collaborative world. In the near future, I believe the elites, including banks, will be hanging on and having to reinvent themselves. Greed and corruption (as we've seen in the GFC and banks here) can't exist in co-operative environments where everyone is equally important; only in hierarchical entities.

Our current education system is ineffective, setting some up for failure. The education system does not yet understand that we are all communicating in a borderless way."

– Alan Rowe, entrepreneur and partner, Vision Business/Barteos

2017, with some amusing digital warnings like: 'No value, no security and no product, just me spending your money. Seriously, don't buy these tokens.' Yet, after 'launch', the UET jokester had made NZ$500,000! The founder then issued a message on the website, thanking everyone investing "regardless of the fact that none of you read any of the warnings on this page". After reading the FAQ answers, I believe they unwittingly contributed to his personal wealth.

Creative with Money rule #3: Look for ways your money can actually grow, with the least amount of risk.

The trouble with all this cryptocurrency trading is: it puts any better, legitimate digitised currency trading system into the same basket for a lot of people. An online consumer can't even tell the difference between unreal promises and an actual peer-based trading system.

Another Type of Crypto Exchange

A local cryptocurrency idea is Barteos tokens, which uses Ethereum (an established cryptocurrency). Initially, it was proposed to enable the exchange of goods and services with small vendors around the world. But it has not gone very far, after some initial problems.

The makers said the use of Barteos on the blockchain has had many technical improvements that allow the token to be transacted in a few seconds, scalability, speed, and transaction costs of US 3 cents each. This compares favourably with other token trade costs.

Why the Fascination with Crypto-Currency?

What about buying into Barteos? To participate in their new launch, you need to have Bitcoin or Ethereum. This means that you are risking a more popular crypto coin and your underlying paper currency on an unproven one, albeit at a cheap level. The value of a functional trading currency like this is based on the number of retailers offering it as a way to pay. With Bartercard withdrawing from its deal with Southern Logistics (Barteos backers), it's not looking so good for them.

Plus, because all the other blockchain currencies are being traded for their own sake, new people to this concept just don't 'get it'. This is why the people factor is important in these types of innovations. Unfortunately, the people working on the crypto start-ups seem to under-estimate the amount of resources and partnerships they will need to succeed.

Although we can see the dangers with unproven currencies on the blockchain, I love the philosophy of a decentralised trading system that benefits all parties and is Government compliant.

Time will tell whether any coin or token system will work and alter the way we can transact in business.

Other Creative Ways to Exchange Services and Products

Since starting in 1991, Bartercard members have saved $4.5 billion by taking cash out of the picture. While most exchanges involve small amounts and include cleaning, accounting, furniture, air conditioning repair, and more, there are also larger purchase trades done with property and resort holidays.

Property trades is a big one. There was a 40 percent increase in the value of Bartercard real estate sales in 2018—in other words, properties with a cashless component of 'trade dollars' in the price tag. To earn trade dollars, members simply welcome customers on Bartercard, after joining the program.

The average trade dollar component in the properties sold last financial year was 30 percent, however, a record $2 million development block in D'Aguilar, Brisbane sold without any cash in the price tag. Shortly after, a $600,000 development block in Bundaberg sold in the same way.

The Bartercard Property website contains about 240 listings, collectively valued at nearly $140 million. (Source: Bartercard news.)

My Opinion

With a 20-40 percent trade value component in most real estate buys, it might represent good value if your professional business is ready to sell and exchange but you're finding it hard to sell. The thing to keep in mind is that an 11 percent Bartercard service fee in cash—plus the usual GST (Goods & Services Tax) within the trade—is still due on a successful purchase. Ask the account manager for help with understanding these.

I have personally used Bartercard to help me exchange some copywriting services for other services. Well, a little. People who use Bartercard to sell businesses and buy another one are definitely thinking creatively how they can offer a win-win solution. It makes me wonder what other trades we could negotiate on, without the need for a formal trading platform.

Tip: Also try your local Facebook 'swap services' group for a free way to trade services as an introduction or swap items no longer used.

Lending to Peers

When considering long-term savings, we need to get more creative and consider new avenues to achieve better returns. These days there are so many partly self-funded retirees barely getting by, with poor returns from their bank deposits. But why settle for 2 percent?

With peer-to-peer lending, investors receive fixed annual or monthly payments that matched borrowers make on loans… and get an attractive return. In fact, the top rate from Ratesetter is 7.8 percent for a 5-year term (although you can get early access, for a fee). The other options are three-year fixed (4.5 percent) and one-month rolling. Considering our inflation rates, the capital would earn about 3 to 6 percent over inflation.

Ratesetter is a UK and Australian peer lender with a 10-year track record. It offers their investors compensation and security with a Provision Fund. This has meant that when any missed payments happen, the investor is covered by the buffer fund (which currently stands at about $15 million). So far, 100% of current investors have got their money back, although they do stipulate that the investment carries risk. They also screen new lenders for creditworthiness and they pay an amount into the provision fund to match their credit score.

Borrower repayments can be automatically reinvested back into the relevant lending market, helping investors earn returns on both their initial principal and the interest earned.

Alternatively, investors can choose to withdraw either the whole amount or just the interest portion of borrower repayments to their nominated bank account, giving them something to live off.

What an amazing modern solution to the problem of living in a low-interest-rate age.

Why the Fascination with Crypto-Currency?

6.
In Search of Income

"The job market doesn't care about your hopes, objectives, passions or plans. It only cares about the value you bring and the problems you can solve" – Christy Frank, Stand Out and Succeed

Unfortunately, it seems that people who don't currently make enough money to be comfortable are the most vulnerable to claims of better earnings. Such was the case after the launch of Uber and Ola, who blitzed the market with ads for new drivers. In 2013, these two driver app companies actually offered reasonable pay. Drivers told the Times of India that they'd been promised monthly incomes of about $1,500—a really good income for an Indian, some of whom have little education. But with the huge influx of willing drivers coming from farming or university students, there were many drivers competing for few rides. Around 1.5 million Indians now drive a car for Uber, Ola or another company.[18]

In May 2018, Indians driving for Uber went on a country-wide strike. Why? Because they are barely surviving: most are in huge debt from lending the money for the car, on contract. After paying almost US$7 a day for car debt and commissions, hard-working drivers might earn the equivalent of US$3 a day. Tied up in this debt bind, they cannot see a way out.[18]

To make matters worse, share ride companies used to take a 10 percent cut from each ride, but now it's about 30 percent. This is also true in Australia, where Uber take 25 percent. In addition, drivers are forced to charge rates that are fixed by the app company (often subject to discounts) and bear no relation to the car costs.

Uber drivers in Australia, having gone through the fear of fines, are currently earning around $15 an hour on average after fees and maintenance.[19] This is $10 less an hour than working in retail sales at an Aldi's supermarket, except at Aldi's you aren't expected to maintain a modern car in pristine condition. Nor do you incur extra costs, like GST, car insurance, and traffic fines.

This form of self-employment is also overly controlled, unlike your own business. Never expect any ride-sharing or delivery company to be in full support of contractors they use. They really don't care if the contractor earns enough for their costs or borrowings.

Uber Eats deliveries is the latest way for students and others to earn some money. However, it was reported that their average wage earnt has recently gone down to $13 per hour, so the riders say, while two people say their work amounted to $5 an hour.

Past driver, Mr Gupta, said companies like Uber "tweak their contracts to make it look like workers are independent contractors (so) their rights can be exploited". He also claimed that their app tells them to go longer routes, while the company did not pay for anything but the shortest route taken.[20]

An interesting story about the merits of the gig economy in New Zealand was on TV while I was there. Some common themes arose. As you're a contractor, what about your taxes, KiwiSaver, insurance against public liability, and petrol to get around? A lot of underemployed workers take on side gigs that ostensibly helps them save for something, but there is quite a lot to cover, considering the low pay.

Another aspect is the drivers are not getting any surety of income. One day a driver earned $150 from rides and other days less.

One more problem: if you hurt yourself while gig-working then there is no sick pay, as you are classed as a contractor.

In Australia, some companies have been investigated by the Office of Fair Work to ensure they are not treating employees as contractors. Employees have to go to work at certain times, but contractors should be able to negotiate when they work and have several client hirers.

If the person contracting is not paid the equivalent or more to the award rate, this is also a red flag. In 2019, a Gold Coast Pizza Hut was fined for not paying a delivery driver the correct award rate and doing 'sham contracting': 'For reasons including the level of direction, supervision and control Zhao and his company had over the driver—and because the driver was not genuinely operating his own delivery business'.[21]

The problem with parlaying other countries' competitive, low-bid systems onto our economic landscape is that Australians have twice the costs and plenty of regulations. Does the gig purchaser have any idea that their proffered $100 for bond cleaning a four-room house will not sustain someone in an Australian city who has to travel there, work four hours, and pay for equipment… and at the same time, I wonder if the gig worker has done the maths?

When you are figuring out ways to earn an income, do you want it to be one-off work that is just labour… advice that adds value… or a digital product that you can sell again and again?

Alternative to Driving or Bicycle Food Delivery:

If you drive every day, you could get around $100 a month for wrap advertising on your own car, says The Penny Hoarder website. They advise to not reply to any car advertising opportunity elsewhere, as some are scams designed to make you pay for the car wrap while their own cheque bounces! Cheeky.

Wrappli (http://www.wrappli.com.au/) operates in Australia. Earn $200 to $600 per month.

Carvertise (https://carvertise.com/drivers/) covers the USA.

An Uber driver in the United States? American company *Viewswagen* will let US drivers do in-car advertising, earning them about $3 an hour more than the $14-16 an hour they currently earn.

Don't Hit the Income Ceiling on Your Way Up

Perhaps you focus solely on income… but your most precious resource is time, not money. Time—and our energy each day—is definitely limited.

If you are in a low-income job and the people above you don't have the success that you dream of, then there is no real incentive to improve, get promoted and stay. With time being limited, you'll probably need a new strategy!

If you're a middle-income employee or soloist, work out how much your earning ceiling is if you:

Work 40, but bill 20 hours per week @ $100 per hour x 42 weeks per year (consulting): $84,000

Work 40 hours per week @ $35 per hour x 52 weeks per year (wage earner): $72,800

You can see that while the employee earns less, the small difference would likely be eaten up in the costs of doing business, and the risk of income fluctuation is all on you.

Time Available x Hourly Pay = Time Ceiling Limit, OR

Sell Product x % profit x % of market = Market Limit

Author product x % commission x number sold less costs = Royalties

Yes, you can probably work out that a Market Limit is the best kind of limit. You can work like a dog, but here is the kicker: when you are employed or self-employed, your income is limited to your time — and if you stop working, the money stops flowing in. That's why passive (or residual) income is sought after by the rich... because once set up correctly, it works for you all the time.

Sales commission or royalties are also good because that stream is not tied to time; it's tied to your results. Royalties can be a tiny reward though, for a huge time input up-front.

Lack of Time?

Some who complain about lack of time and a poor income seem to spend their non-working hours in a way that mimics a toddler playing in a sandpit. Social media newsfeed rubbernecking, shopping for a one-off occasion, whiling away the hours watching reality TV… are just some of the ways adults spend their spare time.

But perhaps I'm being unfair. According to a NAB wellbeing survey, many Australians say that lack of time is detracting from their personal wellbeing. Indeed, one University of Melbourne professor says we are "highly time-stressed compared with some other comparable countries".[22]

This lack of spare time costs a fair bit of disposal income too. Survey respondents who outsourced chores regularly paid an average of $88 a month on cleaning, $53 a month on gardening and home maintenance, and $34 a month on car washing.

The survey also found that young women between 18 and 29 did 10 hours more housework/child-care per week than males of that age, and were willing to spend up to $134 an hour just to win back an hour in their time-pressured day.[22]

While Millennials often turn to outsourcing tasks on AirTasker to save 'time', there are other creative ways to gain back your time. If a young woman has a family and also works, then her spouse should be:
- Picking up and dropping off any kids to care on a rostered basis (fitting in with work schedules)

- Doing their own washing, dry cleaning and ironing—unless this is part of an agreed exchange for the partner doing chores, like all the gardening
- Also checking on the bank account, bills, and expense budget regularly, unless not mentally capable of doing so.

It's nice then, when one partner does a favour for the other of doing their washing or checking their oil—and not a role requirement. Have a talk about roles and what you and your partner are comfortable doing… not to have a gripe, but so you can score roughly the same free time (not free with your kids at your feet, but really free). Equality between the sexes means equal spare time, not just equal pay and equal work roles.

It does matter to your future what you do with your 'spare' time. If you procrastinate, like many of us do, it can eat into your current earnings and future profits. Rather than writing ten books in ten years, there are writers I know who spent a decade writing ONE book. Opportunities and trends are flying past at break-neck pace, and you need to work fast to catch them. Part-time, it should take around six months to research and write a book, depending on length, with another two months spent editing and typesetting.

You, a Vlogger? Why Not?!

If you have a passable video recorder (a modern phone or a videocam) and you love to explain some area of life or business, then you could create a niche YouTube channel with what you've found. Once reaching 1,000 subscribers and 4,000 watch hours, you can monetise the videos through either YouTube advertising sponsorship or have links to affiliated tools (and sign up for the commission).

What's needed for ongoing popularity? Enthusiasm for your topic area, knowledge of popular YouTube 'keyword searches' and how to place these keywords, and plenty of creative ideas. Some friends willing to view the videos wouldn't hurt, either.

If this high number of followers is daunting, then try writing articles instead. The limits on pay-outs via **Medium.com** is low (just cents) and it's based on share of premium reader revenue. While only 8 percent of Medium partner writers earned over US$100 in 2019, there is a chance of earning an extra $500-1,500 per month if writing consistently popular content.

Whether you like writing or prefer a video cam or paintbrush, never let all your spare time be squandered. Relaxing is necessary some nights, but a couple of times a week there is usually a few hours you can spare to develop your skills. I took up an Applied Business course at University, online. A home-sitter I knew spent some evenings doing brain training and her weekends selling niche pet products at the markets. Savvy!

Counter the Computer or Smartphone Time Suck:

Join **TimeRescue.com** and use their mobile or desktop app to monitor your website usage. Every week, view the report and really have a look at what you spent your time on. Any business administrative tasks might be better outsourced, or perhaps you could just spend less social time on Facebook. Whatever it is, look at time as your precious gold.

Develop Yourself with Training and Education

One thing to remember every year, when thinking of extending your career, is to ask yourself: how can I develop myself this year? While others wait for a promotion, it is not about what an employer can supply for you; it is about what you can do to make yourself a more valuable commodity.

If you are in a service business, doing specialist training or adding certifications should increase the amount you can charge (if your skills and credibility also rise). Sometimes a professional association, professional indemnity insurance, or certification may allow your company to take on Government contracts. There is now a Digital Marketplace in Australia to match Government contracts with suppliers, if you happen to be in the digital specialist agency space.

Leveraging your creative skills can happen in practically any field. Whether it's turning a project of making a cubby house into a cubby building business, or turning your spare outdoor room into an AirBnB stay, that aim can take you from pure passion to a planned income.

Build Your Personal Brand Authority

If you want to build your authority as a thought leader and you can write fairly well, you might choose to write and sell your own book via online bookstore channels. Alternatively, if it's eBook only, you could give it away to prospective customers. I've done both, and there is nothing like the credibility that emanates from publishing a quality, printed book.

However, selling eBooks may be nice, but this small revenue is not the main aim of the game. It is a far reach to be among the 0.06% or other of Amazon authors that make 1,000 sales, but if not this, then it is a good idea to build authority in the area you want to inhabit. And I believe that serious fiction writing is probably best done through a publisher and not on your own, for this very reason.

Professional photography and graphics also contribute to your personal brand. You can charge more if all of your copy, photography, website, products, and so on look or sound professional. Good reason to find better suppliers, yes?

Read more on business brand in Chapter 13.

7.
Find your Hidden Bank Vault, with Unclaimed Funds

Did you know that as you move houses, you could be leaving money behind you in an unseen and wasteful trail? Take this time to do a little digging and find hidden bank accounts, shares, lost Superannuation, and possibly even unclaimed estates of relatives.

About $1.2 billion in unclaimed funds is available from old bank accounts, shares, investments and life insurance policies now matured, say ASIC.

Not from Australia? Look into all the kinds of unclaimed fund returns and rebates in your home country.

What Happens with Unclaimed Bank Accounts?

Unclaimed money received by ASIC (Australian Securities & Investments Commission) is transferred to the Commonwealth of Australia Consolidated Revenue Fund, but is available for claim at any time by the proper owner.

To claim, you will need to supply some credentials, such as a TFN and date of birth, and the details of your search result.

Different types of funds are governed by different rules. Bank accounts become 'unclaimed' after seven years if the account is inactive and is over $500 (with no deposits or withdrawals).

So, if you are looking for old bank account money, then see ASIC MoneySmart's Unclaimed Money Search. Some figures below $500 will be held by the actual bank or another financial service. Don't forget to type in your previous full name, if you changed your name by marriage or deed poll.

Other Types of Money Claims

According to The Office of State Revenue, NSW: 'Unclaimed money' is cash "greater than $100 held in an account which has been inactive for at least six years." Then it is passed in to the Office of State Revenue.

In Australia, we can search and claim directly at the Trustees' office or the Treasury office in our State. The type of unclaimed monies that can be searched may include:

- dividends, salaries and wages
- rent and rental bonds
- trust money, over-payments
- principal and interest payments
- refunds
- deposits / premiums
- expenses
- royalties and commissions
- debentures, bonds, convertible notes and
- proceeds of sale.

Claim Lost Shares and Investments at: *https://www.moneysmart.gov.au/tools-and-resources/find-unclaimed-money/claim-money-from-shares-and-investments.*

Superannuation becomes unclaimed after five years of inactivity by the member (i.e. the company has lost all contact with the member) and no contributions have been received for at least two years. Deceased members' superannuation also becomes unclaimed by other parties when "the superannuation provider, after reasonable efforts and time, cannot ensure the benefit is received by the person entitled to receive it." (NSW Office of State Revenue)

Most unclaimed superannuation is held by the ATO. Rather than going through an intermediary, you can now claim your own lost Super through the secure website at MyGov.

All the state government agencies hold different types of money. For example, The NSW Office of State Revenue also holds New South Wales (NSW) Public Sector Superannuation. Here is a list of all State Trustees of Australia, where you can do Unclaimed Money searches.

ACT - Public Trustee and Guardian for the ACT

NSW - NSW Trustee and Guardian

Northern Territory - Northern Territory Office of the Public Trustee

Queensland - Public Trustee of Queensland

South Australia - Public Trustee South Australia

Tasmania - Public Trustee Tasmania

Victoria - State Trustees Victoria

Western Australia - Public Trustee Western Australia

Claim Back Commissions

Have you ever bought an insurance, superannuation or mortgage through a financial planner or broker? You could retrieve the trailing commission through: YourShare.com.au.

Similarly, Americans often pay trailer fees (or up-front load fees) when investing in mutual funds. These trailer fees range from 0.25 to 1% per year and actually motivate financial advisors to recommend that their clients invest in a particular mutual fund. You can't change what's past, but you can opt to invest in index funds (passively run funds which track a particular index) or ETFs (exchange traded funds), in line with your intended risk. These charge from 0.04-0.09% expense ratio, which is a lot lower than mutual funds.

What about an Unclaimed Estate?

Lots of people have died and left their assets behind, having lost touch with relatives. This is called dying 'intestate'. If there was no will and no probate granted and you're a relative, you might have a shot at claiming the estate assets. But you'll need to provide ASIC with certain information about your personal details and relationships.

Since 2009, first cousins can also apply to unclaimed estates, but they wait behind brothers, sisters, parents, children, spouses, and grandparents.

See ASIC instructions for claiming **intestate estates:** *https://www.moneysmart.gov.au/tools-and-resources/find-unclaimed-money/claim-money-from-shares-and-investments.*

8.

Fearful Investors

Being creative with money means you're the one making the strategic decisions and hiring accounting, legal and lending professionals, not being dragged into others' schemes. It means you do your own due diligence on each buying decision. It certainly does not mean you chase passive income at any cost. This only leads to shattered dreams.

Investors generally use borrowings—a valid wealth vehicle—and their deposit, in order to make gains and income. They also usually start with an asset base (usually a property), which helps them get the loans.

In Australia, most successful property investors have succeeded with various strategies, e.g.:

- renovate and flip (sell within six months)
- creative sub-division (e.g. get a D.A. and split the block in two or three titles)
- small development (e.g. build a townhouse on land) or
- buy well and hold, many times over.

This success has been buoyed by the increasing demand for houses or apartments close to an urban centre, investors chasing gains, and of course the whole development sales market. The amazing property gains in Melbourne and Sydney over the past 15 years was driven by more demand than supply... although being cyclic, there is always a lull or backwards step for a while and so growth is never linear.

When demand slows for new developments and builders start to have trouble with financing and selling, this is probably the time to leave it a couple of years until the recovery is underway. This way, the worst of the doldrums is over and economic signs are positive, giving a more solid footing for new investors.

Some investor educators make their own rules in any climate. Regular Queensland Top 100 Rich-listers, Kevin and Kathy Young, rose again from the ashes in 2016. Having been declared insolvent with The Investor Club in 2014/15, they started The Property Club two years later: same stuff, different name. Why let some terrible client experiences in the past and a lawsuit spoil their money-making?

You see, one group of investors in 2007 claimed that their Investor Club-sold luxury apartment investments were valued under the price sold by a matter of $500,000 each unit. The group of investors from WA found that asset amounts on lending documents had been 'fudged'. The real value of apartments in Kirribilli Heights were only ever worth less than half of the $1.2 million stated.[23]

In 2014, the Youngs were again sued by a NSW couple, who said that they were told to sign blank forms to purchase four properties. The Investor Club (or TIC) then allegedly falsified their joint income on the loan documents (adding $250,000 to their minimal income of $50,000). To keep the properties, the couple had to pour money into the outgoings, only questioning it when the money kept flowing out. The couple lost their savings, had to sell their business and came close to losing their house.[23]

Perhaps not all members have been wronged, especially since investors who have multiple properties have the capacity to wait any temporary setbacks out. New investors though, don't have this cushion, nor do they know of the enormous sales commissions and potential over-valuations.

Mr Young freely admits his staff members give advice but do not hold a financial services licence 'as they don't need one'.[23] Does all that sound like the actions of a company you'd trust your life savings with?

The Property Club earns 5 percent commission, paid by vendors. In the past, 'The Investor Club' was found by the courts to be doing the work of a real estate agent and earning from both the buying and selling transactions in the same deal: an illegal practice in Queensland.

A buyer's agent and a vendor's agent can co-operate on a property transaction; however, they must be from two different companies.

This is roughly how it works at educational investment property companies:

Carried away with the magic words and social proof from members, most people attending these seminars are not aware of the bias behind an entity that both educates on investing and sells people the properties. If new developments are sold, the company takes a commission on the sale from the developer… this could be around 10%, which is hiding in the price. In some places, the company may hire a conveyancer and market valuer to collude to ensure nobody knows the real market value of the units sold.

Or if this is not quite the way they work, then the educational company may step in to be a 'buyer's agent' and charge from $7,000 - $10,000 to the buyer to negotiate a deal… usually on a duplex, apartment or townhouse in a little-known development that is hardly the buy of the century. This could be on top of any membership fees you might be paying for some personal mentoring and perhaps best-case-scenario spreadsheets.

The unrealistic dreams sold at these types of property seminars include all kinds of dumb ideas:

The promise of capital gains where there really is no room to move: the price is at a high or is over-priced due to extra commissions and backroom deals.

The promise of capital gains in an area where there is plenty of land, on the outskirts, e.g. on-selling it in a few years for a capital gain, except demand is not high there.

Lending at your upper limits on the basis of negative gearing tax breaks and current interest rates (all-time lows), both which can change and affect cash flow drastically.

Buying luxury apartments off the plan in the hopes to sell it to a more clueless buyer for a gain; but often the market moves in the opposite direction by that time.

Why do we get Fooled?

The optimistic investor in us hopes that someone in the financial services/investing business has the right plan and can lead us to wealth within ten years. Many in the seminar crowds are in their fifties or sixties and want to create an income stream before they retire. Fair enough. According to the seminar, it seems as if novices could use their 'simple strategy' to buy first one property, then another in two years, and another, and gain by this leverage and projected growth over time.

Many of these people are not at all greedy; they are just looking for a faster way than their super contributions or a simpler path than worrying over equity choices.

As ever, there's no better way than researching carefully and finding the best value investments yourself. One way you can do this is by practising.

The ASX Sharemarket Game lets you practise choosing company shares, 'buying' and 'selling'… and see what happens without losing any real money. I've done it and it lets you suffer no illusions that you're the next Warren Buffet. Keeping up with the top players is a real challenge and helps keep our expectations in the field of reality. See Asx.com.au/education.

Interesting points about CFD Trading

What about taking bets on the direction of financial markets (indices), shares, forex and commodities? About 13 years ago, the most prevalent trading derivative became Contracts for Difference, or CFD Trading.

This trading is highly leveraged, meaning the contracts can go either way (up or down)—and the leverage is from 20 to 400 times. (If you know anything about leverage, that alone should scare you). It's so risky that some countries ban this type of trading.

Fearful Investors

The companies invested through are not safe either. During the period 2008-2015, there was:

- Global Trader Europe collapse (15 million pounds owing)
- Sonray Capital Markets collapse ($65 million collapse)
- MF Global collapse (left $300 million of investor funds in limbo)

It seems to me that, each decade or so, a new way to 'make money' comes along: or a set of shiny new shovels to dig the fool's gold with.

Mortgage Trusts / Debentures / Unsecured Notes

Cloaked in many different names, these debentures and notes offer senior investors a high fixed-income investment in mortgages... which sounds safe, doesn't it? But there are hidden traps... this finance props up new property developments, often utilising a high-risk financing strategy called mezzanine financing.

ASIC's MoneySmart says: "Debentures, secured and unsecured notes are unlisted investments. This means they can't be traded on a secondary market like the Australian Securities Exchange (ASX). So it is very difficult to sell them if you decide you no longer want the investment."

If the project fails, you may lose everything you invested. ASIC advise to check their benchmarks document to assess risks, which you can see at the investments part of their website. You can also Google the name of the company and its product name and look for comments from unbiased onlookers.

Horror examples from the past:

- Australian Capital Reserve (lost $330 million of investors' money)
- EquitiTrust (debts $700 million)
- Provident Capital (In June 2012, their $120 million debenture fund was frozen)
- City Pacific (debts $100 million)
- Allco Finance Group (debt of $1.1 billion), Centro Properties and MFS (investors fight to recover losses in court in a class action for non-disclosure)
- Westpoint
- Prime Trust
- LM Investment Management (bankrupt in Australia)

Creative with Money Rule #4: *Only invest after researching on your own, checking out performance and reviews.*

New Concepts—Same Old Story

Jamie McIntyre always had a gift for explaining things simply. Options: "renting shares"; Warrants: "betting on the future". He was an early promoter of financial education, sending out free videos or DVDs: a lead magnet for his highly-priced financial courses. The Eminis trading course had various levels, and students each paid from $5,000 up to $30,000 in course fees and mentoring. Many lost even more than this on trading.[24]

I know it was over-priced because I worked for a direct mail publisher who published an informative 28-lesson financial education course in the mid-'90s for about $500, or $20 per lesson.

Particularly interesting is that although Jamie McIntyre exited his Eminis Trading Platform in 2014, it didn't take him long to find a new way to rake it in. He was grilled at a Senate hearing in 2015 over a delayed Shepparton land-banking scheme, where many investors were duped of their money on the false promises of strong returns. McIntyre was then banned from corporate life for a decade by the Australian Securities & Investments Commission, following a Federal Court fight.[24]

He didn't seem to understand the ban, carrying on with promoting gimmicky ideas in Australia while residing on the Isle of Capri. He says in the advertising that Aussies can 'make $5,000 to $10,000 per month in semi-passive income'. The latest idea is to rent out tenancies at weekly market rent then hire them out as fancy weekend stays through AirBnB, at inflated prices, like $595 per night.

Obviously, this contravenes AirBnB policies as well as the concept of a fair go. He actually advertised the McIntyre family's own $4.75 million mansion on AirBnB for $791 a night.[25]

9.
You: An Empowered Investor

There are particular things you can do to move yourself along towards being financially stable and independent. Whenever stepping into investment, however, lots of misconceptions seem to arise. First we'll discuss investing small amounts into stocks or funds, and next we'll uncover the love affair we have with property. This infatuation sometimes clouds our judgement about the vagaries of the property markets and the risk of investing with leverage.

Investing in Company Shares (Stocks)

Now to investing in public companies and sharemarket indexes. If you love a gamble, then get used to losing on the stock exchange… but if you approach it with more research and strategy, then you could do better than okay.

The main benefit of investing in equities and indexes over direct property is liquidity. Meaning, you can sell when you please. Another benefit is you can get in at a much smaller level and pay a lot less to be a player. Just a few dollars is all the 'entry fee' is to invest in ETFs.

A small downside is: most people do not leverage into stocks and funds like they do when they 'buy' (borrow) on real estate. You can, with margin lending available at around 60% of the equity's value, but most don't. And this means that investors also don't get that power of compounding from a larger amount.

If you plan on investing in stocks, invest in five or more. Out of five companies, expect one to be an abysmal failure. The middle three will perform about average. And one lucky one just might overachieve the index average by a margin of 30 percent or more. While these are general averages and each investor may have a sounder or less sound knowledge of what is a valuable company to invest in, this guideline helps you understand the odds.

Exchange Traded Funds (ETFs) and Index Funds

If you don't have enough money to comfortably invest in five companies, then look at ETFs. ETFs are a diversified portfolio of securities (shares) which mimic a particular index (or market segment) and are bought on a stock exchange.

Index funds also track the performance of a particular market. Both ETFs and Index funds attract much lower fees than managed funds (as low as 0.14%) and are more cost efficient than holding groups of shares.

They can also help you invest where a small investor normally wouldn't. If the Top 100 companies in a major exchange like the ASX is doing poorly, perhaps emerging economies in other countries are doing better. Of course, there is an ETF for that. Diversity of assets is a very good idea for investors, as it spreads your risk.

Selling an ETF is also a quick process: it does not need to wait for a certain price to hit.

Brokerage fees apply when buying/selling ETFs on the sharemarket, whereas contributions to a traditional index fund do not attract any fees and you can top up at will. That said, you'll soon see how to get started with ETFs at low cost.

Learn more about ETFs at Vanguard, Morningstar, or the like.

Save when Buying and Selling Shares or Funds

Normally, every time you buy or sell shares or ETFs, about $20 flutters out the window in brokerage fees. For frequent sellers, it all adds up, and eats into any profits. Investing portals (apps) like Raiz or Sharesies are now available to keep investors from losing lots on brokerage. They might have a tiny account fee, but their fees are nothing near the $100 or so you could easily spend buying and selling a few securities or ETFs each year. Raiz charges $2.50 per month (under $10,000) or 2.75% for over $10K, and that's it.

Depending on what you buy, the usual fund management fee (0.3-0.9%) could also apply.

Some Australians worry about paying Capital Gains Tax. CGT could be payable on 100 percent of the sale, if the share sale means a capital gain. But if you keep the share or fund for more than one year, only 50 percent capital gains tax is payable, at your taxable rate. If the sale means a loss, that loss may be offset against any other capital gains that you make that year (but ask your accountant for details).

With the smart apps at the end of this chapter, you can invest in small parcels of funds while keeping to your strategy and ethical investing values.

Do your Due Diligence

When you hear of an investing opportunity, where do you go? Do you just take it on face value? In Australia, go to ASX.com.au and look at the company's charts and reports, or for US shares, go to Bloomberg.com. Can't find them there? Then look on Wikipedia and TrustPilot to garner their background.

There was a time that I just took my friend's word for it; that this was a great idea to invest. But that experience in being a fool was enough for me to now take some time to consider all angles of a so-called investment before jumping in.

Here are some questions you can ask yourself as you dig around:

- What is the company's track record and share price record? Have they been around longer than a fart?
- What are the distributions/return forecasted for the next two years?
- Is the percentage return forecasted feasible? (3-10% p.a. is feasible; 30+% p.a. not feasible)
- Can you see physically what they are building, or is it pie in the sky?
- What does our Government think of any untested technology/other investments? Is it on board?
- How does the investment rate in risk alongside your other investments? Could you simply put more into a safer investment already paying a good yield?

These are all valid things to consider before investing a dollar or a coin. Even Bitcoin contains your real fiat currency, and what you'll get back is not guaranteed.

Knowing the past and current distributions and profits forecast by market analysts will rule out pure speculative buys, because if a company is not issuing a distribution (a payment for shareholders), it is not bringing in much, if any, profit. You can find all this out on any major stockbroking platform or on your country's stockmarket index website.

Look up pricing for the year-to-date and past two years, and adding the distributions together, work out the dividend yield.

Tip! Don't buy at the highest price it has ever been at and query the reason if it is the lowest price the stock has ever been at. Something might be going on that is alerted to in recent news or from stories of disgruntled customers.

Exchange Traded Funds—or ETFs—are a good way to get started in equities investing. In the next chapter, we'll look at strategic ways to invest without getting duped.

∽

Your Groceries = Company Shares (Australia)

Having trouble affording any extra for equities? A new start-up in Australia gave shoppers 2% of their grocery spend at Woolworths, Coles, and IGA as a micro-buy into the public company they shopped at. For instance, I spent $244 and got $5 worth of Woolworths shares under their management. There are no fees.

Their new system will link to your shopping rewards card. Your micro shares also earn distributions (free money on top of free money!)

Halo Money rebranded to Upstreet and will re-start in May 2020. See *https://upstreet.co/*

Earn Stocks for Shopping (US)

Bumped offers a micro investment scheme for loyalty shopping. After downloading the app (iOS or Android), you'll be asked to link a debit or credit card you normally use to make purchases. Then once you spend money at a participating retailer, Bumped will reward you from 1 to 5 percent of your spend with a partial share from the company. Bumped has passed FINRA's broker check. *https://bumped.com/*

Buy Shares with Zero Commission (US)

Robinhood is an upcoming app that will help US investors do self-directed trades in stock or cryptocurrency on app or web. Offers fractional shares – in other words, invest your spare change. Among the first to offer zero commission on buying/selling US-listed and other securities, including ETFs. No account fees but there may be other fees, e.g. for wire transfers or margin lends. *https://robinhood.com/*

Buy Micro Shares (Australia/NZ)

Use a micro investing app to get started on an investment portfolio.

CommSec Pocket is a new investment app by CBA's investment arm. It has low brokerage fees of $2 each and minimum investment requirements of $50 - $61. The app lets you invest in seven different ETFs, e.g. Aussie Top 200, Global 100. The advantage here is the ability to check into each ETF, with the quality information and risk level chart, including tips. It has no account fees and the usual internal ETF management fees of 0.09 – 0.67%.

It draws on the information from online broker, CommSec.com.au. This full website lists their usual brokerage fees (brokerage rates between $10 and $29), so indeed $2 is a bargain.

Raiz is another choice of micro-investing app in Australia and it lets you invest 'spare change' automatically or make recurring investments. Start with $5 or a lump sum. There are no sell fees. You invest into a pool of ETFs and choose one of eight portfolios. So, more diversity still. You are not charged a brokerage, but it's $2.50 a month to run the account ($30 a year). Source: Finder.com.au.

Sharesies is the New Zealand equivalent to these apps, and you can pick from several bundles, including socially responsible funds and New Zealand or global ETFs. Sharesies has a choice: a fee of NZ$1.50-$3 a month for accounts over $50, or $30 p.a.

Investing in individual companies will incur another charge (0.5% for under/0.1% for over $3,000). You can invest from $10 per week, or one-off investments of $50 on up.

These apps allow you to automate your micro-investing buys and reduce your brokerage commissions. Don't forget to check what returns funds are getting and if the price the funds are now at seems like a good price this year. That said, investing monthly will mean the share buys are varied in price across different times, thus reducing the risk of buying high in bulk.

You: An Empowered Investor

10.

Property Investing Outside-the-Box

While thousands of eager Aussie and New Zealand investors have gotten on board the property investing train, a good proportion of them hardly leave the station. To get to the next station of wealth, investors need two things: capital growth and good cash-flow.

To get capital growth in the near term, they must have bought on or under market value, not over. Plus, the purchase needs to have some good timing in the cycle. Plus, a good location, close to schools, major roadways, shopping centres, and not too far from employment hubs. So many things to get right and all must be done with a cool head, with facts and figures.

To get good cash-flow, they must know all their costs and work out the best case, worst case, and most likely scenario. Part of this is calculating repayments when interest rates are 2 percent higher than present rates. This is to check your serviceability is okay. It's also thinking through what would happen if you lost your job or your tenant leaves with no notice.

Needless to say, many new investors get roped into investing inside a seminar where only the best-case scenario avails and some costs are never mentioned at all. "No capital required, use OPM, no skills needed" are often touted. Of course, paid-off home equity is your capital and your non-earning asset. It is what you've worked so hard to accumulate.

Property Markets Move in Each Direction

A usual line trotted out by property strategists is that property doubles every ten years, or goes up at an average of 10 percent. But do all property markets rise by 10 percent every year?

According to a recent chart from CoreLogic, three regions of Australia show dwelling values lower than they were a decade ago. These regions are Perth (-6.9%), regional Queensland (-5.1%) and regional WA (-29.5%). So, that answers the question above. Usually, some areas go backwards, others forward by a bound, and others stand still. You can't very well project any particular property will grow by an 'average' rate.

Now for an anecdote to illustrate exactly that. In the 1990s, some investors got caught in the stagnation period. My mother and I purchased a 3-bedroom house in Nelson, New Zealand for $150,000 in 1993. By 2000, our family had to sell up to pay other debts. The now 4-bedroom, improved house sold for a meagre $155,000. In the next two years, guess what happened? The price of houses went up about $100,000 in that area.

Do property cycles last for 8-10 years? It depends on the general economy. Sometimes the economic boom lasts for two years and the crash and recovery lasts a long nine years. The spread is eclectic, although it is always a cycle.

> 1990-1993: we had a 'classic' economic crash, with an unemployment peak of 11%

2008-10: property prices dove; business was down: fallout of the global financial crisis

2019: at least four news articles mention 'slowdown/softening coming our way'

There are a lot of machinations going on behind the scenes of up/down house prices, business confidence, and credit expansions. Chief Economist for Australian Institute of Company Directors, Stephen Walters, said in a speech in 2016 that national income had been shrinking since the end of the mining investment boom and that the government needed to make a new agenda for reform and help lift productivity if Australia was to recover. But with lots of political leader instability, it never happened.

Then, in June 2019, AMP chief economist Shane Oliver confirmed that "the outlook for 2020 looks challenging". The risk of a recession for Australia in 2020 is now 25 per cent, he told ABC News. Another economist pointed out that household income lagged company profits, so wages as a share of GDP was at 51.8 percent, close to a multi-decade low.[26]

With all economic cycles, as with this one, the only thing that's sure about it is that a recession (or contraction) will happen at some point. Brace yourself!

Why Not Negative Cash Flow?

Negative gearing means paying for more costs than you get in income in any year. Our country's rules mean investors get tax breaks for these losses on investment, which applies when the investor is a salary or wage earner.

Negative cash flow is a result of the savings on tax being not enough to offset all the costs.

While a high earner may be able to pay for a few years of negative cash-flow out of their wages and hope for that growth, most of us middle earners (on the borderline of serviceability) need to clear the path for future investing. Thus, we'd aim to spread the risks across several properties. And for this, we'd need a solid annual yield.

After all, few lenders will lend more money when your current investment is costing some of your wages already—what with capital growth being uncertain. No matter how well you budget, lenders will only lend to a certain percentage of your (and any partner's) earnings. So, the higher the rental yield and the fewer costs you need to pay, the more easily you can service a loan. If interest and costs eat into your cash inflows too much, those lenders are going to deny the application next time you want to invest.

What is rental yield?

This yield is a percentage per year that the investment makes after costs (but not after personal tax).

Gross rental yield is your annual rent income divided by your property's value.

Net rental yield takes into account the total property expenses, including stamp duty, legal fees, loan fees, building inspections, repairs and maintenance, management fees, insurance costs and other rates and charges.

What is a Good Gross Rental Yield for Residential Property?

Australia	UK	USA
5.5%	7 - 8%	4.4 - 7%

Sources: US: GlobalPropertyGuide.com; UK: https://www.property-investmentsuk.co.uk; Aust: https://www.smartpropertyinvestment.com.au/research/18895-what-is-a-good-rental-yield

For those wanting to have a solid cash-flow and thus looking at yield as a deciding factor, Commonwealth Bank considers a good rental yield on residential property 5.5 percent or over. This is because if it is under 4 percent, then it may represent over-valued property. It is not a hard and fast rule of course. The average rental yield for a unit in Sydney is currently 3.1 percent, while a unit in Brisbane is a more attractive 5.3 percent.

Why Not Invest Heavily in Residential Property?

Residential property investors have to pay the rates, the maintenance, any renovations, repairs, home insurance, landlord's insurance, and bank interest. These costs often eat right through the rental income and start on your own income.

There are other added risks (or rewards), depending on the location you invest in and the vagaries of the surrounding industry. Some investors lost heavily after buying houses in small mining towns, like Emerald, Queensland, where the entire town was affected by a pullback of mining activity.

Renovation adds smaller risks, of over-capitalising or over-committing your income or time. The potential upside is there too, but more likely in a buoyant market and with experienced renovators.

With domestic investing, renters can also move out after six months legally, leaving you starting all over again looking for someone, all while paying out. All repairs are paid by the landlord.

In most states, investors have to pay an enormous amount of stamp duty when buying and this makes investors reticent to sell, even if their property suddenly turns out for the worse. Holding a dud property for years on end really eats into your potential to invest in better things, which is called 'opportunity cost'. So, let's now discuss a less popular alternative.

Why Commercial Property?

Commercial property investors, on the other hand, have more assurances and less costs. There is the major cost of interest to cover, major maintenance, sometimes strata fees, water infrastructure and council rates, all depending on the lease terms. Investors might plan an initial renovation to encourage a solid lease, but equally they could encourage the tenant to take care of that if it benefits them. The commercial tenant will pay for most other small costs.

So, even if there are higher interest rates to get a low doc loan (say 1.5 percent higher than average), if a net yield of 9 percent is coming in, then there is usually plenty of cash left for you. A net yield is the percentage of cash returned after costs like water, rates and insurance have come out. It does not consider your income taxes or land tax on the taxable value of your freehold land (amounts vary).

You can judge roughly the cash flow by calculating the difference between the interest rate on a typical commercial loan and the net yield stated by the agent. But to get right into the figures, you'll need a more sophisticated investment cash flow spreadsheet, including depreciation and loan costs particular to a planned purchase.

The amount you'll spend as a small commercial investor depends on your situation, but you can get business premises (some tenanted) in Australia from $200,000 on up.

There is also a risk. The risk is that if your tenant moves out, there could be quite some time with a vacant building and costs mounting. This is why the longer the lease and the more solid the tenant (national is good), the better off a new investor is, risk wise.

Larger deposit needed

One drawback is that in these days of tighter lending, many lenders want to see a 30-35 percent deposit on commercial property, particularly from those with a SMSF (Self-Managed Super Fund). This deposit usually comes from a drawn-down on home equity through refinancing an investor's primary home. That portion is loan no.1, with a regular variable interest rate, and the remainder is a commercial loan at commercial loan rates.

Some non-bank lenders will let you get a higher loan-to-value ratio, e.g. 75 percent (allowing 25 percent from home equity) along with making it less about the investor's wages and more about the property income source (*source*: Bedrock Funding).

But the good thing about commercial properties is, once the lease is read through and a solicitor has approved, the tenants are vetted and settled and the diligence period is finished, the property becomes a 'set and forget' investment for around three or five or ten years — when the lease expires.

Just before lease expiry, savvy investors negotiate a way to raise the rental price while keeping all the good benefits the tenant wants. How? Well, you pick up the phone, armed with latest market rents in the area, and negotiate. What do you want as improvement? is a good starting question. Pretty simple, right?

Generally, national and reputable business tenants are not going to do a runner, but even if they do, there is a usually a lease clause for that eventuality. They must pay that rent by law, unless in total liquidation. However, it's important to have a property law expert check the lease beforehand.

Though some landlords find it hard to attract a tenant in between leases, once they get a stable one, they are often there for many years. This can be because they put a lot of their own money into its beautification or their brand becomes part of the place. You'll need some advice on comparative values and tenant risks before investing.

An Aussie expert in commercial property cash-flow, Helen Tarrant, recommends you buy a commercial property (leased out) that is a net yield of 8 per cent or more. This is because, she says, when the bank tests your serviceability, the gap of about 3 percent satisfies the mortgage manager that the property is self-supporting... covering principal and interest repayments well and truly and giving a positive return.

You can learn a lot more about investing for cash-flow from her online education in commercial property and free eBook. (www.helentarrant.com.au).

Management Rights

For those who already have money in shares, then your next step might be to think of: who could go halves in a small investment in commercial property with me?

One particular option is a 'management rights' deal at a smaller level. This is where you rent out and manage units on behalf of the body corporate or motel owners. If you happen to have a licensed letting agent as a friend or partner, then would they be interested in a joint venture? You could live there, look after lawn mowing, and open up to new apartment tenants. The letting licence for this costs a lot, plus they would do checks on tenants, so they would deserve at least half the income.

Alternatively, you can study to get your own residential letting agent's license at your state's Real Estate Institute, who offer online learning and training manuals. After finishing the course, you still have to pass the Government's screening, and pay nigh on $1,500 for one year to Fair Trading for the operating license. You must also register an office at the block you manage and open a trust account for tenant payments.

The investment in a management rights agreement for apartments ranges from $250,000 to over $1.2 million, which at the middle and top-end normally includes a residence. Sometimes it is a business premises that you would attain rights for.

The total remuneration varies wildly (from $50,000 to

$155,000), and some just list 'net income' so be sure to know all the cost expectations that may come out of the income.

To find opportunities, search "Management rights for sale [place you live]". You, the rights holder, must live close by and be willing to work a few hours a week as you'll no doubt be visiting often, if you don't actually live there.

Banks are much stricter with lending requirements so if you want to be a novice in commercial holdings, look for a 'non-bank' lender to fund it.

Most letting managers don't stop at one property to manage; they add more to add income. To do this well, most have an office, a computer and answering machine, a tenancy database check, and a network of reliable tradies to help manage the residences.

Resources:

Land tax: *https://www.qld.gov.au/environment/land/tax/calculation/value*

Stamp duty calculator: *http://www.procommercial.com.au/stamp-duty-calculator*

Commercial real estate search: *https://www.realcommercial.com.au/for-sale/* (Filter by tenanted type: tenanted)

11.

Spending Less and Saving $10,000

Sometimes, no... most times, we spend unconsciously, and this is often to satisfy not just our physical needs but our emotional needs. After all, a drink of tap water (filtered) satisfies your thirst for about 5 cents. Why bother then with a $4 coffee or chai latte? It's all about emotional payoffs. (I still like the odd chai latte and I realise why).

Don't forget that high street retailers and online merchants are wise to pricing products that play to our desires and emotions. One cognitive bias, called Weber's Law, is about perceptions. The law states that the change in a stimulus that will be just noticeable is a constant ratio of the original stimulus. Although price gaps can vary, the price we notice is usually more than 10 percent. We don't notice changes under this.[27]

Now, I'm not an expert in psychological principles, but I believe this is how price setting plays out. One day, my husband called me up all excited and says he found a Hisense TV on an incredible sale: $595—or $300 off the marked price. While he was on the phone, I Googled the make, model and size. Out of the five stores displaying the LED, 4K resolution, 55" TV, only one was dearer than this price, one was slightly cheaper (online) and the rest were the same. After I told him this, the flame went out of his urgency to buy. It does seem a bargain at the moment, considering the original price for a television of that type in

2016 was $1,499. But that's just a factor of technology moving on rapidly.

My bigger point is, what bright future are you forgoing just to satisfy your emotional triggers? For some, they can easily afford the niceties of life, but for those of us who struggle to save for our important wealth goals, it is a much harder question to reconcile.

How to Save $10,000 to Invest Later

How much nett salary has passed through your fingers over the last ten years? $500,000? $1 million? (Remember, this is salary or drawings after income tax). If you think about it this way and come out with a big figure, it sends packing all those excuses that you never have any money to invest!

$10,000 can buy:

Only 100 pairs of $100 shoes, or

400 $25 books, or

365 Lattes, 106 muffins, 48 $8 lunches, 52 $3 cold drinks, 12 months of Foxtel basic, 40 unplanned take-aways, and monthly artificial nails... the fripperies of life.

I'm not saying it's easy to save $10,000. It certainly isn't. But, with tracking, you can see how quickly it slips through your fingers.

You also can't rely on willpower and having spare money at the end of the month or fortnight. Instead, put in place some good money habits that will keep on going and make a big difference over time.

Spending Tracker Apps

One of these good habits is watching your spending. There are many spending trackers on the market which allow you to categorise and watch your actual budget, but some are phone incompatible or out of our geographic zone.

A useful Australian mobile app for saving and tracking is Pocketbook, which is an ideal budgeting tool if you swipe or tap to pay mostly. I found my credit union and connected securely to it, to track our spending digitally. In five seconds, it had categorised many of our monthly spends and while a few needed some help from me, it's a fast way to see what you've spent on say, groceries or fuel. It's safely spend option can help you budget your categories (it's an option).

For those elsewhere, there is Wallet, for Android. (There is a Wallet app for iOS, but this stores payment cards). Besides tracking spending in a customised budget, the goals tracker part of Wallet will allow you to set a timeline and money goal, with suggested monthly amounts towards it. Setting reminders means you don't forget your goal and once all set up in Wallet, you can view the next 7 days' of your money life. No, it's not psychic; besides tracking past bills, you can also put in planned payments.

I had a goal to pay for a dental bridge and rather than putting it on time payment plan (which has fees and may impinge on uncertain finances), I decided to save up for it. The app told me how much I needed to save monthly (or weekly) to make my goal by deadline. It can remind me to keep on saving—as long as I use the app. Setting a regular day and time to check on your budget is a good idea.

If you don't like the thought of joining up your bank account to an app, then another free spending tracker I used a few years ago is a website-based tracker called BudgetPulse. You just export your banking account details to QIF or CSV while on internet banking, and categorise your major areas, like Groceries or Clothing & Shoes. It's fairly manual though.

For a free tool, BudgetPulse is very good with visuals—with two ways to view your spend categories and over-spending! Unfortunately, I forgot to put the mortgage payment in manually: a rookie error. Because that account was not one I tracked, I needed to put each payment in manually. See *www.budgetpulse.com*.

Quicken is faster for set-up and use, with its automatic category filling, although it's around $35-45 a year for membership. Quicken works on Mac, Windows, iPhone, Android, and their website, so plenty of choices for how to use it. See *www.quicken.com*.

A second good habit is prioritising saving for your future, over the fripperies of life.

How Much Should I Save?

The simplest way to find out a savings figure is to first add up all regular bills and arrange to pay most of them monthly. Don't forget home maintenance and car registration. After working out the sub-total, divide by 12 to get monthly amounts. Put all these monthly amounts in your spreadsheet or personal finance software, or if patient, find out after 12 months of using a spending app. After mortgage/rent and bills, and accounting for all income, what are you left with?

That number is your discretionary spend, or 'gap'. Discretionary includes new frypans and fridge updating. Don't forget gifts, whether it's for your family or your child's friends. What about holidays? And snacks on the way to work? Magazines or Books? Wow... I bet you didn't realise just how many categories there are that you control.

Now you have to start prioritising by putting your savings first. If unencumbered by debt, put a portion (e.g. 15%) of your income/expenses gap into an online savings account, automated to transfer in the first 2 days after 'payday', or 'drawings day' if self-employed. If you have consumer debt, then put as much of the discretionary spend as possible automatically and monthly into repaying that debt.

Don't forget to still pay 9 to 11 percent of nett earnings into retirement savings (also automatically) and put aside estimated personal tax, if you do run a small business. Monitoring what you spend in your business is also very important, as costs can quickly gobble up revenue.

What to do with the $10,000

Once you have squirrelled away your first $10K, you might now realise how hard saving is and to be very careful with it. You're stuck—where will it go now?

Here is a rough guideline, but your path will differ depending on your amount of debt.

The first $3,000: keep in an interest-bearing account for a floating emergency fund.

The second $3,000: Getting rid of any consumer debt is next, particularly if it's over a 12 percent interest rate. Pay later deals or cards are based on the stupid assumption that someone will have more money spare later, next month or next year. Even if you do, there is always a course or a replacement computer to spend it on. Pay it off.

You could also choose to put this $3,000 into your home mortgage, particularly if your debt level is high. It's a safe way to get ahead and save on interest.

The remainder: If it's your first investment, then consider a diverse ETF or index fund. Consider a 'smart beta' or other ETF across a range of the top 200 companies, for instance. (See the apps in chapter 9).

For those who like acronyms, here is one that's easy to remember.

SPEND LESS

S: **Stop** buying on impulse. Wait 24 hours before buying items over $100. You are going to think it over and probably will come up with a cheaper, perhaps recycled solution.

P: **Plan** your shopping trips and online purchases—ensure it fits in your budget.

E: **Eradicate** bad spending habits, like always getting a new dress for every event.

N: **New**—it doesn't always have to be new. Two-year-old cars encounter less depreciation but are still modern enough feature-wise and less polluting than old ones. A table and chairs that are sturdy but are sold preloved may well last for ten years.

D: **Design** your financial goals around your life goals.

L-E-S-S: You get to make up this part.

Creative with Money rule #5: Always spend less than you earn... and have a 'rainy day' fund

Spending Less and Saving $10,000

12.
Pick Your Cash-Flow Quadrant

Like many of the Amway business owners staring bug-eyed at Robert Kiyosaki and his whiteboard up on stage, in 1998 I was green to the concept of the investor and business-owner mindset. (Please forgive me for joining Network21 and Amway).

I thought then that self-employed and business owners were one and the same. But using Kiyosaki's Cashflow Quadrant®, it's easy to grasp that being in the Employment and Self-employed zones (left-hand side) is hamster wheel stuff. Not necessarily always, but in the vast majority.

In the B (business owner) and I (investor) zones is where it gets really exciting for rare entrepreneurs. Rare because, according to Kiyosaki, "very, very few" self-employed or small business people ever turn into what he terms as business owners (with 500+ employees or financially independent). But, Kiyosaki says the way to business is not from the E (employment) quadrant either; after all, you need the practical skills and focussed mindset of being a smaller business first. (The Midas Touch, 2011).

Maybe, but there are a few chickens who didn't take this particular path to the coop. Biz Stone co-founded Twitter, and he came from mucking around with design, websites, and then podcasting. Similarly, Sean D'Souza has built a solid revenue business in Psychotactics (marketing strategy for small business), working creatively, largely by himself. Not everyone must become a CEO to profit well from a business idea.

Part of this inability to grow a small empire is how we approach business. Most of us do not start off with a business degree with an entrepreneurship focus. Most of us are not surrounded by other successful business builders or professional investors, like Kiyosaki was, so we don't pick up the right focus. We don't concern ourselves with leadership skills and brand management because we focus only on our specialty, our job. We're not thinking about building multiple product revenues. We either have our specialist career or we get stuck in that place of wanting flexibility but not earning enough through freelance gigs.

This is why professional development, personal development, and even business school is very important for anyone starting a new business that is not a franchise.

Creative with Money rule #6: Pick a Quadrant and then a specific vehicle

Creative Business or Investing Ideas

Applying the Cash-flow Quadrant to our life, have a think about taking one of two paths:

1. Stay employed in profession and learn a leveraged investment strategy in the weekends. Then invest or jointly invest after your due diligence.

2. Grow a self-started business into a brand that sells your Intellectual Property or collated information in one of these ways:
   - niche training courses
   - subscription membership model
   - certification in being a facilitator of your methods
   - retreat based on your topic, with 2-3 speakers
   - personality tests

Sometimes it's hard to turn our creative side back on when we've been hustling in the day job or business. That's why it's good to do a few mind exercises first. The act of putting pen to paper or marker to whiteboard seems to help the creative process. Brainstorming on a select topic is ideal, but first feed your mind by looking at all different styles of businesses. Have a read of Smartcompany.com.au/startupsmart or Entrepreneur.com.

We'll be going over some of these ways and giving you starter ideas soon.

Outside the Quadrant?

We love the Business and Investor paths, but there are a few areas not easily defined by the quadrant: high-growth start-ups and solo entrepreneurs/educators. People like Michael Hyatt and Brendon Burchard don't exactly fit the mould; they are in business, but they are right in it and are building a tribe directly. Unlike Richard Branson, who builds businesses through his company managers, brands, etc.

What role do you want to play? What level of safety do you need at the age you are? What resources and assets do you have? These answers all play a part in your decision on which path to focus on for income creation and wealth building.

Another way that's a little different to conventional business is to sell your private coaching. Business coaching, life coaching, and specialty coaching is a huge industry and there is no cap on what you can charge, apart from ensuring the demand for it. So, if your expertise has real value for others and your advice provides shortcuts and tools that they would take years to discover, then why not start out with a service package based on this uniqueness and value. Charging for a block of five sessions and emails is a good way to simplify your offering and put a good dollar figure on it.

Some of us want to go straight from anonymity to selling high-priced courses, but shortcuts don't work, so let's get real about the things we need in place first. Let's talk about earning income from online sources.

Don't Click that Link!

The desire for a more flexible working life leads some parents and carers to try out various multilevel marketing ideas. I have a wonderful friend who has tried seven different Network Marketed concepts. She is getting on board before even understanding whether they are solid ideas, but that's all because of the company's blue sky promises.

Putting time, effort and good money into unproven concepts or top-heavy MLM is wasting good time that you could spend building up your own thing.

Click to Change your Life is a BBC special which outlined just how much money and time hopeful Mums had sunk into an MLM skin-care business, such as Younique or Nuskin. The high-pressured sales environ makes people question themselves: *why am I not going well in this? Should I buy more stuff?* When in reality, 84% of European Younique consultants earnt zero profit for the past month, about 11% earned over €870, while 0.04% earnt over €1000.[28]

Pick Your Cash-Flow Quadrant

13.
Earning 'Passive Income'/Affiliate Income

If you have an interest in creating passive income and you're searching within the 'making money online' field, there are many other pitfalls for the unwary. Psychological principles apply on the Internet and it's even harder to spot the fake people.

Consider this: thanks to the Internet gurus, you may have been conditioned to search for GAIN without much WORK. This leads people into scams, time sucks, or shallow education. It also spells failure for the thousands of people who see others' outward signs of success (income, houses, cars), but don't understand the depth of their drive and action towards their goals. Some gurus neglect to mention the $50,000 or more they invested in their business to grow and market the stuff they now earn recurring revenue from.

Recurring revenue streams from niche-area websites? No direct contact with customers, only automated marketing? It sounds like a dream way to build profits. Some people say you can make lots of passive income from affiliate income websites, but this is clearly not something you can do on day one of learning.

Some people teach others how to make 'semi-automated

income' from importing products and selling them on Amazon or other shopping platforms. But are those goods in your area of passion and expertise; your Ikigai? Online educators have a team to do some of the difficult technical work needed. Will that be your support? If there are 100 other students, can you be the first to market?

After all, it is the ability to find a new concept people love, along with a firm dedication to marketing it, that will make the business a winner. Online creators who excel in niche market research, copywriting, magnetic marketing, and who have a keen eye for profits seem to be the more successful ones.

It takes a lot of knowledge in many areas to get all this to work. Whether ecommerce or subscription or affiliate businesses, it's no place for a technophobe. Patience while learning is a good trait to have.

Rather than just a cheaper product or fast-moving item, success also requires a spark of something extra: factor you... your personality and verve. Sharing your motivating reason for starting something new with your audience also works better than pretending to be all perfect and corporate-like. This is because humans relate to each other's stories. We take heart if someone has been through a bunch of obstacles to get where they are today. Perhaps we might be able to do that too, we think.

Steering Clear of the Gurus

Our faith in authority figures sometimes leads us to fall into money traps. Research into obedience to authority has shown we are strongly inclined to follow the instructions of someone who looks like an expert. We will even substitute our judgement for those with symbols of authority. The research shows that we even underestimate the extent to which the appearance of authority will influence us.

While the old scientific tests were mainly done with people in doctor's coats, this influence also applies to financial experts, marketing mavens, or any authority figure. This is probably why anonymous marketers use famous, credible people to advertise courses on Facebook.

So, what can we do about it? How do we detach ourselves from this strong influence and work to our own goals?

One way is to forget the social proof, forget the bloated income graphs, and make your own decisions. Arm yourself with the right research on a niche market that's not too competitive or too broad.

Use specific data from good data sources, not from specific marketers. Some good data sources include peer-reviewed journals (though hard to read), in-depth books by niche experts, and case studies in high-level podcasts.

Doing a Simple 'Side Hustle'

Finding a good side project takes a lot more than just jumping on the latest hot thing or opening a digital marketing service (please, no, not another one)! If you are not wanting to risk much capital on a business, then running an online magazine, course, or membership full of helpful information on a specific topic can pay off—for the patient types.

This is because people are willing to pay for information that guides them to their goals and dreams. Not because it is not available online, but because it would take too much seeking,

Earning 'Passive Income'/Affiliate Income

verifying, and ensuring relevance to your own cause from the masses of information available.

It is better if you have taken a certain path and now provide a shortcut or series of solid steps that will work for a novice.

First Step: Deciding what you are going to market

Research is part of any successful enterprise, so let's explore some of the most searched for and evergreen topics on the internet. I have taken out the irrelevant or unethical, to give you some starter topic ideas:

Business – entrepreneurship is huge; real founder interviews; specific tips

Computers and mobile devices – share your own reviews, comparisons, and shortcuts

Hotels/travel information – competitive! Try a travel blog with amazing pictures

Real Estate – how to get started with renovating/flips, small developments, coops, etc

Small business marketing – how to run ad campaigns, best marketing platforms, WordPress training, social media image sets (product), Instagram success, etc.

Adult education – all manner of topics, hosted on an online platform like Teachable, Thinkific or Yescourse.

Photography – how to take amazing photos, camera talk, Instagram tips

Flowers – about flowers or how to arrange them

Health – also think yoga, massage therapy, nutrition, etc

Music and learning to play instruments

Work from home jobs – run a website listing real jobs or creative freelance pursuits and home-based business articles

Within one of these popular topics, you will surely find a connection; something you love to do and what others enjoy too. Then you can start attracting people through your written words and the tips you want to share with others. There are a few more details to learn, but finding a valuable market in your area of interest is at the heart of it.

Gather intelligence on competitors in the niche and list them in a simple table, along with their social follower numbers. What is their unique proposition? What is their marketing saying: energy, beauty, healthier, younger, wiser, richer? What is their level of pricing (a clue to market positioning)?

After searching and noting lots, you should be able to see what kind of creative site and information you might want to make to fill a perceived gap. Remember, information (or t-shirt designs) is much easier to package and sell than actual products.

Tip! Selling products on a unique domain is not super viable for newbies… because it's really tough competition. Do you have $20 million to compete with Amazon?

Second Step: Getting Your Online Ducks in a Row

Next, if you want to create informational content online, find a domain name for your business—and a business name! You'll need to search the online domain registers for vacant names and also search ABN.org or similar to search for vacant business names. All the while, search Google for your preferred name (try .com.au and .com). If what comes up is very similar and also extremely reputable, perhaps have a second think.

You have a good name; memorable but not too hard to spell? Good, let's now get either website hosting or procure a self-hosted website.

For side projects, it's perhaps not worth wading through all the learning and plugin updating that you need with WordPress (which powers 30 percent of the world's websites) unless you'd enjoy that process.

SquareSpace is a program that is easier to run, as websites are hosted by them, and its hosted pages are also quite easy for search engines to find. There are many different templates that can give a brand-you look (change the colours) and it uses a drag-and-drop style builder. SquareSpace personal plan costs around AU$16 a month, while the business plan, with Google Suite and integrations, costs AU$25 a month.

To run a course, some of the platforms are hosted all-in-one platforms. You can use the hosted landing pages to attract people to your course, thus you don't need another website. Teachable and Thinkific let anyone get started with building a course without getting all caught up in technology knots. Just Google 'Teachable vs Thinkific' for a great comparison. You can choose to trial the free plan while testing and building, then basic levels suited for opening the sales doors are $US39 (Teachable) or US$49 (Thinkific) a month.

Next, it's time to see if your chosen web platform tracks visitors. Every month or week, you'll want to check those numbers and make sure there is nothing amiss with the site's indexing or site map. Signing up for Google Analytics and reviewing the reports is free.

After you take care of the technology, it's time for you to collect all the information for your course, membership or magazine. Probably a magazine style blog is the slowest to build up, and you would need to either become a writer or have capacity to employ good writers. If you try to hire cheap writers via the freelancing sites, you might never get a good one. Trust me on this.

A good content writer might live in your local area, already doing something like writing a good blog or writing freelance articles. There is no replacement for someone who knows how to write popular articles and enrich the content with keywords.

Oh, and don't forget to write excellent website copy (or if on a marketplace, write the sales description).

If you can't yet afford a copywriter, then you could do a course to learn more, such as Kate Toon's SEO Success (for general SEO stuff) or the *CopywriteMatters.com.au* masterclass, or others who teach copywriting.

If you feel you cannot learn to write persuasively, then find a copywriter who knows their stuff. Hint: they don't come cheap.

You have a personal email account, right? Well, don't use that for business. Any time someone sees that email address, they could think how unprofessional that seems.

Email addresses are kept at the hosting place, not at the domain name providers. More emails don't cost anything to add, unless you don't already have an account.

For a whole range of tools, you can set up a business email account easily by using Google Suite. You'll be able to auto-forward that business email address straight to Gmail, along with getting 30 GB of storage on Google Drive on Basic plan (US $6/user/month). You'll then be able to access Gmail, Drive, Docs,

Sheets, Slides, Calendar, Hangouts, Forms, and Sites.

The main benefit with using these products over MS Office 365 is live changes and sharing. When a person works on something in 'Docs', they work on the live version. If working with an editor, you can share the link for them to edit directly. So no-one ever ends up writing in the wrong version.

Google Drive is useful for storage of files on the Cloud and is just like Dropbox, although a bit cheaper. If you just want a Google Drive storage upgrade without the rest of the tools, it's $2.50/month ($25 a year) for 100 GB.

At this stage, you should draw up all your monthly costs in a simple Operating Budget. It could include things like business card printing (yearly) and Facebook advertising. It will help to keep in mind the expenses, taxes and profits rather than simply looking at incoming revenue.

Third Step: Determine your Pricing and Test Everything

Mid-way in your planning now, you may be in a dither about pricing. Setting a price for your course or membership (or digital package) is never easy. If you have something you've designed, then check Etsy.com for comparative prices — and don't forget the important factor of how to get it to the customer. If it's a course, look at the courses by lesser known teachers in your new field, rather than the Neil Patel or Gary Vaynerchuck types, who could sell a bucket of ice for $1,000.

You can also test different price points by writing low-budget Facebook ads and sending targeted visitors to different landing pages featuring the info product with three different price points.

If deciding on affiliate links to help along the revenue, then download my Monetization worksheet template at *Creative-Ways-Resources* to get an easy start.

Test your new website. Get a friend or three to test it out on their mobile and laptop. The reason for this is different people on different devices will see it completely differently. At the risk of upsetting you, there will probably be a glaring mistake that you cannot see… and this could cost you regular buyers or repeat visitors. There are User Testing sites that also perform this service, for about $50 a time.

Also test your site's new abilities by sending a contact form email to your new address. See what comes up as a thank-you page and alter if necessary.

Fourth Step: Set up Email Automation

Now it's time to set up email automation for your information site, which is called an autoresponder series. Check out affordable email marketing systems available globally, as you want easy integration with your website or other storefront. Then find out how to send out emails while you're not around, to your slightly interested site visitors.

Perhaps offer subscribers a $10 discount or a free creative downloadable. For me, a handy freelancer rate calculator in Excel worked well to encourage new readers. Utilise a subscriber form which pops up after a pause, or one that asks to notify the visitor of new content.

One that uses 'smart push' notifications is called *Subscribers.com*.

Alternatively, you can just use an email marketing list subscriber form, with a customised graphic, but this doesn't work as well.

If you want to add automation, then try *MailerLite*. From $0 to $15 monthly, EmailToolTester.com says it's the cheapest and simplest for smallish lists. They offer various templates and the extra feature of a landing page (sales page) editor. It's easy to plug into blogging software and its simple and intuitive interface makes it ideal for novices. See *MailerLite.com*

Let's Talk More About Business Brand

'Branding is design that delivers strategy.' – Stephen Younger

Brand, Vision, and Culture is key to a business going places: building something worthwhile that people love to be a part of. Certainly, Hubspot is the master at that, with their free marketing certification courses and tutorials on email marketing. Here's what they say about formalising a vision statement:

> *A vision statement describes where the company aspires to be upon achieving its mission. … a vision statement describes where the company wants a community, or the world, to be as a result of the company's services. – Lindsay Kolowich, Hubspot*

I'm amidst building a brand and community at Business Author Academy, so I often think about my vision for it. A vision is the ethical, win-win relationship and path to growth you see for your idea. A culture is the created vibe of an organisation, that propels each member forward.

What brand, vision, and culture can you create? The venture doesn't have to be just commercial, social enterprises can help part of the world and be financially viable too.

Long Term Business Thinking

When considering the new business, you might tend to nut out the first couple of months. But it is important to think long term.

Using objective thinking, you can plan for the vagaries in the general economy that will affect the ability of your clients to pay you. Instead of worrying endlessly about the tightening purses, try to creatively find a product that is:

- Good value
- Helps others make more money
- Fits neatly into their budget

A do-it-yourself Facebook marketing course that's $200 or on a payment plan would tick all these boxes. The fact is, most people in a sluggish economy do want miracles! But if you can give them at least some good advice they can put in place right away to help their business visibility, then good value is achieved.

Niche in your Area of Expertise

Before going ahead, let's break down all your skills and strengths. I bet you could sit down right now and list out ten life skills you have that will help you earn more income. Go jot them down.

Among this rough list could be a way to make money from

something you have expertise in, but have probably overlooked. For instance, you might have re-written your resumé using several different models and found which one got more results. This might lead to a service, or better still, a more automated website, with special resumé templates and advice videos. (If you like this idea, see a not too dissimilar idea, *MyPerfect Resume.com*, where the initial automated software is free).

This is called a *horizontal* niche; the system is sold to any career person but is particular on the WAY it goes about co-creating your resumé ... something totally new.

A *vertical* niche is a product offering sold to particular segments of target customers, with very different attracting features and benefits for those segments.

The idea with setting up a niche business for cash-flow is using your skills or knowledge to help others get a particular result. If you know of people who are struggling with a better way to… (do anything), then you can find out what is truly needed and come up with a simple offer.

This outcome-driven approach almost always works better than the way most people might think of, e.g. research hot stuff, get a product, promote and sell it online… which is the wrong way to approach building a business income, in my opinion.

To succeed online, you also need to promote the value of your ideas to others. Speak clearly with passion and energy—you never know who's listening.

How to Build an Audience the Authentic Way

People often forget in business that the most revered traits are listening, caring and paying attention. If you show the new prospect or customer that you are doing this for a bigger reason —or simply want to help them achieve a better fitness, a better bank balance, or a better dating life, then that is more convincing. You don't need to add cheesy sayings or flippant slogans.

Online, sharing your story and the stories of others helps create a 'community feel'. It helps people feel confident enough to buy, through the power of social proof, and is not a 'hard sell'. The more personal you can make your marketing images and video, the more traction it will get.

A happy/pretty, or a crazy/energetic, or a thoughtful/helpful persona will get you noticed on social media; whereas dull monologues really won't. Mr Woo is a happy Aussie teacher of mathematics who has grown a large following within YouTube and is known for 'making maths fun' (misterwootube.com).

Don't forget, creating a people network in your business can help you when the time comes that you need it. You'll want to interact and be interested in them first of course.

People you know through social channels like LinkedIn and Facebook may have businesses and some might have target markets (and email lists) that are simpatico with yours. Those that SHARE a target buyer persona (area, income, professions) are perfect to do joint marketing ventures with.

It doesn't need to be via email; it may also involve direct mail, events, and special offers (for both parties, if practical).

Generating Leads Online

Lead generation is always on business owners' minds and with Software-as-a-Service applications, it can be done cheaper than ever before, through devices like:

- Email capture pages or webinar invitations
- Lead surveys (surveys/quizzes containing an email opt-in), e.g. SurveyAnyplace
- Affiliate/Reseller partners
- Free electronic reports, plus email autoresponders
- Blogs (with subscriber requests)

Interestingly, a 2014 study by DemandMetrics.com showed that interactive surveys like apps, assessments, quizzes, and calculators manage to generate two times more conversions than static content, with about 70 percent assessed as doing moderate to well in generating leads.

Someone who blogs and gives away free content is called a content marketer.

An overlooked tool of the content marketer is collaboration, also called reciprocal marketing. This is a non-contractual way in which two businesses can promote each other's content or offers, for mutual benefit. As it is all based on creative offers, it's a free or low-cost way to reach a market. See https://survey-anyplace.com/reciprocal-marketing/ and https://collabosaurus.com/ (a formal way) for two different approaches to this idea.

It doesn't really matter what area you choose, or how big you go, as long as you follow:

Creative with Money rule #7: Your business must be authentic to you and of win-win exchange value.

Don't Struggle Alone

It might seem hard at times, but there is never a need to be alone in business. First of all, because yours is not the only one: there are two million small businesses in Australia. Forums like *FlyingSolo* help connect you to other solo business owners.

HerBusiness.com is a club which helps women business founders learn and keep focussed.

There are also Government supported business coaches/mentors, local business networks or masterminds, and unofficial mentors who may be ready to help you. Some of the ones in Queensland that I've experienced and been happy with are:

- BEC Mentoring for $77 a session
- RDA (Regional Development Australia) run workshops on business growth, branding, marketing topics and provide mentors
- Small Business Solutions TAFE courses, with business mentor as part of it.

Regional Development Australia (non-profit) has 52 committees and their mentors work with community and all levels of Government to support people in business. They are placed wherever you live, so just Google 'RDA' and your general area.

In NSW, there is Government-paid mentoring for people starting or expanding a small business.

See *https://business-connect-register.industry.nsw.gov.au*

Earning 'Passive Income'/Affiliate Income

14.

Design your Life Goals by the Number

Perhaps you see money flow as simply a source of fun or a necessary exchange, something that you have no real control over. A-ha, but you do.

Perhaps you've heard of Maslow's hierarchy of needs, which is based on the theory that you must meet your basic needs first, social needs and love, before you can reach for self-actualisation. In a similar vein, let's take a look at my hierarchy of money needs.

Hierarchy of Money Needs

If you're barely surviving, it doesn't mean you're on an unemployment pension and drinking whisky from the bottle. It could be that you have $30,000 in credit card debt with only a $50,000 a year (after tax) job. If there always seems to be more bills than there is income to pay it, that's survival level. Acceptance is the first step before making plans to move on.

Next level up is surety of income. That's where you have a regular income and are able to meet your family's main needs, but have to juggle and save up if you want luxuries, like the latest gadgets or boating type hobbies. Some here will not manage well if losing their job or business, if saving has not been a habit and cutting back never thought of.

Income 'in excess of needs' is where there is at least $10,000 every year over your budgeted spends (not including fripperies). Here, you'll feel like you have some choices and can go on an annual holiday or buy a car. These people are often the ones to write into *Money* magazine, as although they might have funds in investments, they're concerned over their long-term financial wellbeing.

The exciting level of gifting and dreams is also called 'financial independence'. Breaking through is possible only after moving through the other levels… although there is no guarantee that this move will be permanent. An income of more than double or triple your budgeted needs leaves you with plenty for donations, gifts, hobbies, or trips to foreign locales.

Most people at this level know exactly what is coming in and going out (having a higher money consciousness) and usually put the acquisition of real assets first. For instance, they are building a business up. This means that they are very unlikely to buy a Mercedes on the first year they earn double; instead, they buy an income-producing investment. This investment could pay for their dream car later… after compound growth does its magic.

Which level are you on and where are you headed next? It's important to realise you need to travel through the stages, both in mindset and in real income, to get to the top.

You also need to be comfortable (and not guilty) about what you have and earn. Some lottery winners find themselves back to their usual comfort level two years after they win, reflecting the valuable part that mindset plays. If you start to consider yourself as lucky and savvy, this will help with reframing your thoughts around receiving more money.

Paying attention to your life goals and finances, particularly if done together with your spouse, will help you get to the next level. On your own, it's a viable challenge but some might need the help of a wise buddy or coach. Let's start with some basic steps.

Track your Life Goals

If you've got life goals to fulfil, either download ASIC's Track-MyGoals app (on both iOS and Android) or just write your top five goals this year on a whiteboard. Remember to put both a number and a deadline on each goal. Whiteboards are better because they are there in your face every day, whereas notebooks are often left, forgotten, in a drawer.

Updating my family financial statement and goals every six months has been a good way to keep track of our small progress towards financial independence and paying off our mortgage. The steps have been slow, not because we spend voraciously, but because we work for ourselves and so both have an income tied to general business confidence.

Reaching our goals is also slow due to mortgage interest. Never fear, you and I are in this battle to pay off debt, spend wisely, and increase income together. With more focus, we can do it!

Proving the power of automated savings, we made progress with an education fund for our daughter, added to over a period of ten years. It's heartening to see the progress towards our initial goal made possible by small monthly amounts and bonus interest. (Some youth saver accounts have a higher rate of interest than usual). With higher education expenses adding up, a starter $10,000 account for all those text books and transport costs will help.

Tip: If you plan to fund your child's education from your mortgage offset, this is not such a feasible idea because you likely don't want to go backwards on the mortgage later, when drawing it out.

No matter what age we are, we must not forget that one day we'll want to retire. Working in a business, it's all too easy to forget to put aside some retirement savings. I had been putting across a pittance every month for ten years before I realised that it should be at least 10 percent of my taxable income (i.e. after costs). Recently I doubled the amount; after all, a nice retirement has to be more important than a fancier mobile phone.

I designed a Family Financial Statement form to help my readers, and a fresh copy is in the resources pack at https://www.jenniferlancaster.com.au/creativeways-resources. You just fill it out with your personal income/funds/savings numbers.

No matter what your life goals are, they will come to fruition much easier if you put a number and a date on them.

Design your Life Goals by the Number

15.
Don't Worry, Age is Just a Number

Imagine you're sitting at your desk one day and your boss (or client) comes in and says, "You now have to manage on one-third of what you've been getting. I hope you remembered to save".

Welcome to a retirement without thoughtful planning. It's not cricket, is it, when you find out that your right to the age pension has been creeping slowly away from you... as costs of living steadily rise.

Then *future you* looks at the retirement account and finds it has eaten a lot of your contributions in fees and poor fund allocations. Don't let this become your reality.

Typical Age Pensions

Country – Single Age Pension	Weekly equivalent
UK new state age pension	£164.35 / week
UK state age pension (born before 1951/53)	£125.95 / week
Australia pension/supplement/energy sup. Available from age 65.5 to 67 (born after 1957)	$466 / week

US old age pension/social security (The pension is based on the average of the insured's 35 highest years of earnings indexed for past wage inflation, up to age 62.)	$266-$591 max. / week
Supplemental income benefit	$674, means tested
Canada: Old Age retirement pension	$130 / week
Retirement pension plan	$250 / week

Notes:

Australia: Single age pension for residents, weekly, from Sept. 2019. (Lifechoices.com.au)

UK: for those born after 1951 (M), 1953 (F), and contributing to NI for 10 years.

US: Qualifying retirement age is 66 with at least 40 quarters of insurance coverage.

Canada: Full pension from age 65; reduced pension available from 60.

I don't know about you, but these pension rates don't give me of a feeling of security; in fact, they remind me that we are really in charge of our standard of living in old age. Different financial expert sources say we should be stashing away between 10 and 15 percent of our salary towards retirement, although that depends on where you start from.

That's pretty scary when you consider that hundreds of thousands of people are earning short-term type money in the gig economy, freelancing, or running a small business, and (so I've heard) not putting anything much aside. As a business, even if you do the simplest thing and put aside 10 percent of your after-cost earnings in a savings account (for tax), then it is a big step in the right direction. You could also place it into a mortgage 'offset account', as this offsets the interest due on the mortgage.

Besides, creative thinking does not involve relying on the government or the boss, so let's plan now for a retirement with multiple income streams. It's best to do this with our spending in mind—because it doesn't matter how much is earned, if you spend every cent, there will be no golden retirement stream!

Your superannuation (or retirement savings) is worth taking good care of. Aussies can find out how to judge their fund's performance through MoneySmart.gov.au: Superannuation and retirement: Keeping track of lost super. To summarise, they say to compare like funds for like (since some are invested in lower risk allocations), think long term, look for lower administrative fees (because fees really eat into your returns), and find funds that performed better after accounting for fees and tax.

The industry super fund I use charges close to 1 percent in fees and returns have been good, particularly due to some allocations I chose which performed better than Australian shares, e.g. infrastructure. I also keep in mind the inherent risk of each asset class, for example, international shares might give more yield in one year but in other years go backwards.

In North America? Many large US corporations are struggling to meet defined benefit pensions of past employees. With not enough money in company assets, there may not be a steady income in retirement that earlier employees were promised. But with defined contribution plans, the employee is in the driver's seat, with employers sometimes matching contributions.

What's your net worth? Go to your new personal finance software or take out a calculator to find out your current net worth. You'll first need to collect any shares or fund statements, property values, etc, and then calculate loans and credit card amounts. The amount of assets in your name minus your liabilities (loans) is your net worth number.

Once you know this number, you can track it over time. This way, you become more aware of the debt in your life impinging on your wealth, or conversely, the income in your life providing more wealth. Remember, it is better to use a secure budgeting program to track these things, or my simple financial planning form.

Plan a better retirement financially with: https://www.industrysuper.com/calculators-and-tools/calculators/. Find out how much you need in retirement, compare retail to industry funds, find extra money for volunteering to Super (includes give up … coffees per week!), compare Super funds, and calculate your personal income tax.

Tip! Not all employers are diligent with every Guaranteed Super payment, so always check your actual Super account statement against the amount you input into the 'super contribution calculator' you'll find at the website above.

Americans can check out: **TheBalance.com** and its articles on retirement income needs.

Creating Income from a Farm Property

If you're a property owner, you might be wondering: how on earth could I achieve multiple income streams with the land I have?

Well, listen to this true story about a crop farmer's wife, Marcy. When she was 60, she set a goal for herself of getting in $1,000 per week from various home rentals. She knew the age pension just wasn't going to be enough to pay for trips, bills, and everything else.

With a little hard work and the right spirit, she and her husband achieved what many farm retirees would like: an income without debt. Something to pay for health, holidays, and cover the very large utility and insurance bills. Plus, even farmers eventually get too tired to be sitting on tractors all day.

First of all, how ordinary is Marcy? Well, she doesn't know what ROI means and she doesn't ever go to investment seminars. She is a farmer's wife in rural New Zealand, she is a frugal consumer and a generous person. She also knows her town has a ready need for budget accommodation.

Despite dealing with a barrel-load of money worries (business debts and crop failure), she thought creatively to achieve her goal. She managed to squirrel away enough for one Caravan ($10,000) and one relocatable, brown cottage ($10,000 + $2,000 transportation fee). She always had other money saved for emergencies: a lifetime habit.

Over time, she instigated several additions to their growing farm community. For an elderly aunt, she had a garage-to-granny flat conversion done on the main house. Rents for $125 a week.

Hubby's labour, some iron and a few reused windows turned a tin shed into a nice pool flat. Rents for $175 a week. They spruced up an old workers bach (always rented at $100 p.w.) and for more than a decade had one nice tenant firmly placed in an original worker's cottage, paying $150-$190 a week. (Rent rises and still under market a little).

She let no place of abode go to waste: the good caravan was rented out over the summer holidays at $30 per night; the cute, self-contained brown cottage was offered for rent ($200 per week), and the little flat adjoining the main house was offered to pilots for 3 months at a time. A grading shed, previously used to grade tobacco leaves, was converted to a simple flat for people who can't get any other accommodation. It has its own rustic fire for those cold winters. ($100 per week).

The best part is, there is no debt and income is stable. While others worry about economic downturns, interest rate rises or company failures, Marcy (now in aged care) and Jim keep on getting income week after week from their growing community. The total income allows for small outgoings and annual repairs.

And I can tell you for sure that this is a true story, because... Marcy is my mum. I hope this story inspires farmland owners to reframe any misfortune in farming and look around at the opportunities for providing accommodation or farm-stays. Not only them, but anyone with an open mind can see the hidden potential around their home or the reusability of their belongings, and find new ways to earn money.

Creative with Money rule #8: *Plan your retirement to have multiple income streams.*

16.

Some Easy Ways to Save Money

Turn Around Billing Errors

It's all too easy to let each month's utility or phone bill slip under the radar. If you get a higher amount than usual, do you check it? If you sign on a new plan, do you make sure that it is the one you asked for? And do you opt out of paper bills (saving $2.50) and do direct debit (another small saving)?

I changed our account to have no international calls. Next month, I got a phone bill about $25 higher than expected. But, having had no bills for some months, I didn't know why that was. So I sent off an email to a customer member team to get my bill. It came in with a charge for 'Fetch Giant: $23.50'. In our earlier conversation they never mentioned this charge, so I flew into action. I tried the online chat and described my issue. After a long pause, they offered to refund me the Fetch charge and keep me on the low monthly plan. Imagine if I never checked the bill? Yes, you better run and get your past bills now to check for errors.

This bundle (phone, TV box and unlimited internet) plan had been changed a number of times over the years to keep up with the reducing cost (and escalating data limits) of broadband internet. If you've had the same high-value plan for 3 years, you're probably not on the best plan even from your own provider.

Another area to check once a year is your electricity plan, whenever you get that letter that says your contract is up. This year, we stayed with the same provider but I found a plan that was estimated to save around $200 annually in peak energy charges, called 'One Low Rate'. Never let it roll over without looking around, because then your household won't get any discounts or better pricing but you'll still be on a contract!

Just like 'low rate' credit cards and 'basic', low rate home loans, these kinds of plans can save you serious cash. Without all the fancy rewards programs and tricky features, the consumer gets to save cold, hard cash.

The Banks' Sob Story

Did you hear the one about the Australian banks losing millions over the fees that they had to pay back? They printed out their customer statements listing previous unfair fees—but ran out of ink! Poor, poor banks.

Of course, I'm being silly; we should fight back. During the Banking Royal Commission, it was revealed that ANZ allowed customers on Centrelink benefits to carry a negative balance and then charged them up to $60 a month in overdraft fees, as well as 17 per cent interest. But customers were not asked if they wanted the informal overdraft and didn't always know the fees involved. The commission recommended that banks stop charging dishonour fees, overdrawn fees, or allowing informal overdrafts on basic bank accounts.[29]

So, any time you were away overseas and the bank charged you an overdraft fee or overlimit fee, march in there and say you want to see the document stating there is an overdraft on the account. They are supposed to show you this and get you to agree to fees when you join up. You should also not just put up with credit card late fees.

Having won in the High Court regarding late fees in 2016, but chastened lately, ANZ still charges a $20 overlimit or late payment credit card fee and a $6 per day overdrawn fee if the account is $60 or over in debt, up to a maximum of $60. But social security benefit recipients are not charged anymore if they have the Basic Access account. These fees actually cost the bank between 50 cents and $5. What![30]

I urge you to monitor your account spending via your banking app and cut up any high-interest credit card or store credit card. You can use a debit Visa/Mastercard, which only uses your own money, interest free.

AfterPay may be versatile but ensure that you will have the money to pay for the purchase over the next few weeks (after doing your monthly budget).

Fight the Fees when Overseas

We are often caught out with fees when travelling, spending, and getting out cash. *Mozo*, the comparison site, found that the highest foreign credit card exchange fee was 3.65% and the highest ATM withdrawal fee was $5.50. These can really add up if you go to several different countries and hence make many withdrawals.

You can also keep control of your currencies while on holiday and set the currency price by changing it over in advance. A global debit Visa card, like on the list below, can be used almost anywhere in the world and has no foreign exchange or conversion fees, no account fees and no international withdrawal fees.

* Citi Global Currency Account
* HSBC Everyday Global Account
* ING Orange Everyday
* Macquarie Transaction Account and
* UBank USaver Ultra Transaction Account.

There will always be a small difference in rates that you lose when swapping currencies, but this varies between banks and payment portals. You may notice a line called 'currency conversion charge' in your credit or debit card statements after the fact. Also notice if there is a 3 percent or worse rate than FX market rates.

Incensed by these ridiculous fees, I switched all my foreign-billed business expenses to HSBC Global. Now, the account does not show any fees and there is also complete transparency when choosing to transfer money into a currency in advance.

These types of cards make spending in foreign lands much cheaper. You don't have to worry about that extortionate fee or poor exchange rate you're charged when using a 'handy' foreign currency teller at the airport. And you don't get charged those fees travel money cards like to impale on you when setting up or on withdrawal. You can't forget about the money, because it's just like any other bank account you monitor.

Once a customer, download the bank's app to your smartphone for use on the go, if you are good with these. For the

CREATIVE WAYS WITH MONEY

cash-preferred traveller, swapping your currency in a bank of the destination you're going to can be a happy medium, if you land on a weekday. This should not cost you an up-front fee, but it will still take a margin on the conversion rate.

Whatever the case, you never want to use a credit card with no money in it overseas. Used to pushing the cash out button, card owners sometimes forget that any instant cash advance will be charged at the headline interest rate, from the day of purchase, plus any applicable fee. If, rather than cash, you use credit to purchase items, that holiday just got even costlier than it already is by about 15 to 18 percent.

Definitely have a pre-set budget to spend when on holiday and don't be tempted to spend willy-nilly on credit. It's better to have a global cash account handy for emergency purposes and of course take out good travel insurance. If you don't use credit, be prepared to have cash to offer a hotel or rental car agency for a refundable bond.

Tip: When paying online, you may notice that PayPal is giving you a currency swap rate that's 5 percent worse than current rates. I get around part of this by selecting: 'use your bank to handle the purchase' when going through a foreign currency PayPal purchase.

Bonus Tip: If you love travelling in high style but for 14% less than normal, then sign on with Rakuten Kobo and hop-link to Groupon hotels in the city of your intended stay. They have most of the hotel options and offer cancellations. See *Monetization Worksheet Template* on my Resources page for the link.

Conclusion

All this money talk and critical analysis has given our left brain a good workout, hasn't it? Sorry about that. But when it comes to talking about money (even creative ways with it), it's clear that LOGIC must rule over EMOTION if we are to get ahead.

The crazy thing is, we spend so much time worrying over the uncontrollable (the economy or government spending) that we forget we can control plenty of things: our spending, which utility or telco gets our loyalty, whether we pay monthly or quarterly, which bank we use, and what we do with our savings. We can use a brokering app to invest small amounts at extremely low cost, a goal tracker app to remind us of our savings goals, and we can do all this to our own financial plan. What then do we need big bank financial planners or fat cat managed funds for?

A creative money mindset is more about taking time to see what's out there and putting aside other people's opinions. With more education, you'll be able to get out of a generalised state of fear and anxiety over investing, and plan for a rosier future. You'll start to make better money management decisions. Plus, when you focus on your life goals and financial habits, it will become clearer what steps you need to take.

So, whether you are now focussing on earning more in a business (while monitoring costs), or watching your household spending and saving more money each month, it's time to shake things up a little! It's time for you to be in control of your finances. It's time for you to be both critical (to analyse) and creative (to consider new possibilities).

Get started with the free planning resources at: *www.jennifer-lancaster.com.au/creativeways-resources*.

Go your own way!

Value Your Time?

The author has spent ten years learning about how to write, produce, and market a decent non-fiction book. You can now discover her insider advice on creating and publishing your first book.

Take a trial membership at Business Author Academy: www.businessauthoracademy.com [Book Creation Success] for AU$10 (14 days' access).

I'd also love your feedback on the book, wherever you bought it or at Goodreads.

Acknowledgements

A hearty thanks goes to Di Hill for her eagle eye for grammar. Also to Robyn Gulliver, who noted well the lack of structure and topic jumps. I'm also very grateful to my daughter Sarah, who does not enjoy reading about finance and would rather be reading fiction, however, her logic is better than Doctor Spock's.

When you're an indie author, success is in the hands of friends. Everyone who said that they'd like to read the book gave me encouragement to keep going, so a big thanks to you!

About the Author

Along with this book, Jennifer Lancaster is the Australian author of *How to Start a Freelance Business*, *Power Marketing*, *How to Control your Financial Destiny*, and *Create Your New Life of Abundance*. In these short books, she teaches others to market wisely or be mindful of their moolah.

The reason Jen started writing about personal finance is due to her falling into novice traps, such as an off-market stock investing scam. She is a middle-class Mum, with no aspirations for great wealth.

An editor and writing coach for novice non-fiction authors, Jen looks at the meaning behind people's words. She has also written on over 40 topics in both B2B and B2C.

Endnotes

1   Frank Cheung. 'Royal commission suggests criminal charges over 'widespread' fees-for-no-service scandals', News.com.au. 4 Feb 2019

2   Frank Cheung & Sam Clench. 'Banking royal commission's bombshell report: The key recommendations', News.com.au. 4 Feb 2019.

3   Lexy Hamilton-Smith. 'Storm Financial founders fined $140K over 800 million collapse'. ABC.net.au, 22 Mar 2018

4   Michael Janda. ABC Radio National, 'Australians' record debt is making us work longer, spend less'. 18 Oct 2019. https://www.abc.net.au/news/2019-10-18/household-debt-leaves-australians-working-longer-spending-less/11608016

5   Reporter: Alison Caldwell. 'The Brad Cooper Story'. ABC.net.au, 24 July 2002. http://www.abc.net.au/pm/stories/s615703.htm, Accessed 23 Feb 2019.

6   SMH.com.au, 'Superannuation Overhaul presented to Government could add...' https://www.smh.com.au/business/the-economy/superannuation-overhaul-presented-to-government-could-add-500-000-to-some-accounts-20190109-p50qe7.html, Sydney Morning Herald, 10 Jan 2019.

7   Andrew Main. Other People's Money (Rev. and updated ed.). Pymble, NSW: HarperCollins, 2005.

8   The Australian, 'Rodney Adler on jail, redemption... and what he's planning next', 18 April 2015. https://www.theaustralian.com.au/life/weekend-australian-magazine/rodney-adler-on-jail-redemption-and-what-hes-planning-next/news-story/6398ef51e1bc532ccd212a1fd64af228

9   ABC News. 'Uber shares sink on first day of trading.' [online] https://www.abc.net.au/news/2019-05-11/uber-share-prices-plummet-stock-market-debut/11103930 [Accessed 27 Jun. 2019].

10   ABC, 4 Corners. 'The Uber Story'. Aired 18 March 2019. https://www.abc.net.au/4corners/the-uber-story/10912940

11   Sophie Bearman. 'As Bitcoin's Price Plunges, Skeptics Say the Cryptocurrency Has No Value. Here's One Argument for Why They're Wrong.' CNBC, 17 Jan. 2018. www.cnbc.com.

12   Restaurant & Catering Industry Association. Media release: 'Online Delivery Gobbles Up Profits'. Accessed Jan 2020. http://rca.asn.au/rca/wp-content/uploads/2019/12/RAC-Disrupter.pdf

13   AustralianCurriculum.edu.au 'Critical and Creative Thinking'. Accessed Dec 2019. https://www.australiancurriculum.edu.au/f-10-curriculum/general-capabilities/critical-and-creative-thinking/

14   TheNextWeb.com, 'How BitConnect pulled the biggest exit scheme in cryptocurrency'. Accessed 10 March 2019. https://thenextweb.com/hardfork/2018/01/17/bitconnect-bitcoin-scam-cryptocurrency/

15   Sunday Night, 'John Bigatton's role in BitConnect'. Aired 10 March 2019. 7Plus.com.au

16   Mitchell Moos, CryptoSlate. 'Leader of One-Billion-Dollar Cryptocurrency, Pyramid Scam, OneCoin Arrested'. 10 March 2019. https://cryptoslate.com/worse-than-bitconnect-leader-billion-dollar-cryptocurrency-pyramid-scam-onecoin-arrested/

17   United States Department of Justice Attorney's Office, Southern District of New York. One Coin story. Accessed 12 October 2019. https://www.justice.gov/usao-sdny/pr/manhattan-us-attorney-announces-charges-against-leaders-onecoin-multibillion-dollar

18   Amanda Erickson. 'India's Uber drivers went on strike because they're making $3 a day'. March 19, 2018, Washington Post. https://www.washingtonpost.com/news/worldviews/wp/2018/03/19/indias-uber-drivers-went-on-strike-today-because-theyre-making-almost-nothing/

19   Geoff Thompson. 'Uber X Drivers Working for Half the Minimum Wage'. ABC news, 7 Mar 2018. https://www.abc.net.au/news/2018-03-06/uber-x-drivers-working-for-half-the-minimum-wage/9513250

20   Frank Cheung. 'It's Modern Slavery: Uber Eats Drivers Say they Were Paid Equivalent of $5 an Hour'. News.com.au. https://www.news.com.au/finance/work/at-work/its-modern-slavery-uber-eats-drivers-say-they-were-paid-equivalent-of-5-an-hour/news-story

21   Fair Work. '$216,700 in penalties after Pizza Hut franchisee engages in Sham Contracting'. June 2018. https://www.fairwork.gov.au/about-us/news-and-media-releases/2018-media-releases/june-2018/20180615-skyter-penalty

22   Matt Wade. 'Time Pressure is Stressing Us Out'. The Sydney Morning Herald, 6 October 2018. https://www.smh.com.au/business/the-economy/time-pressure-is-stressing-us-out-20181005-p5080i.html

23   ABC News, 'High-Flying Investment Club Sued by Couple'. 5 Sep 2015. https://www.abc.net.au/news/2014-08-12/high-flying-investment-club-sued-by-couple-over-$1m-in-loans/5665976

24   Amy Bainbridge and Suzanne Dredge. 'Would-Be Traders Lose Thousands on Spruiker's Program.' ABC News, June 2014. See: www.abc.net.au/news/2014-06-06/dozens-of-australians-lose-money-through-financial-education/5506654.

25   Rateek Chatterje, 'Property Spruiker Jamie McIntyre's Airbnb Play under Scrutiny'. PropertyObserver.com.au, Jan 2017. https://www.

propertyobserver.com.au/forward-planning/investment-strategy/property-news-and-insights/64053-property-spruiker-jamie-mcintyre-s-airbnb-play-under-scrutiny.html

26   Stephen Letts and Michael Janda. 'Australia's economy slows to levels last seen during the GFC'. ABC News, 5 Jun 2019. https://www.abc.net.au/news/2019-06-05/australian-economy-slows-to-levels-last-seen-in-gfc/11180688

27   HelpScout.com. Pricing Strategies. https://www.helpscout.com/blog/pricing-strategies/ [Accesssed Nov 2019]

28   ABC Four Corners. 'Click to Change your Life'. BBC program, aired 28 October 2019

29   Clancy Yeates. 'ANZ Bank Wins in High Court Bank Fee Case'. The Sydney Morning Herald, 27 July 2016, www.smh.com.au/business/banking-and-finance/anz-bank-wins-in-high-court-bank-fee-case-20160726-gqdzj8.html.

30   Charis Chang. 'The Most Outrageous Bank Fees'. News.com.au, 7 Sept. 2019. www.news.com.au/finance/money/costs/bank-fees-the-hidden-costs-you-may-not-even-know-youre-paying/news-story/.

Other Sources:

Callan, Gallois, Noller and Kashima (1991). Social Psychology. 2nd ed. Harcourt Australia, pp.100-104.

The Next Recession: https://fbe.unimelb.edu.au/exchange/edition2/the-next-recession

What is a Good Rental Yield, Australia. https://www.smartpropertyinvestment.com.au/research/18895-what-is-a-good-rental-yield

What is a Good Rental Yield, UK. https://www.propertyinvestmentsuk.co.uk/how-to-work-out-rental-yield/

CREATIVE WAYS WITH MONEY